TROUT FISHING
WISCONSIN
SPRING PONDS

TROUT FISHING WISCONSIN SPRING PONDS

By Christopher Deubler

Drawings by Dan Hansen

Siskiwit Press

Published by: Siskiwit Press
2606 School Street
Two Rivers, WI 54241

ISBN: 0-9654303-0-8
LCCN: 96-92605

Drawings by Dan Hansen

DEDICATION

To the memories of my sister, Amy,

who taught me some valuable lessons about life,

and my grandfather, Joseph E. Wood,

who sparked my interest in trout fishing.

ACKNOWLEDGMENTS

First of all, I would like to thank my wife, Ellen, who has put up with all the time I have spent writing, typing, and editing this book and also for all the days I have spent traveling around the state over the past several years in search of spring ponds and information about these ponds.

During the early days of gathering information about trout waters, I would like to thank Hans Pearson of Silver Lake College with whom I was able to coordinate my research efforts. Paul Peeters, a state fishery manager, at that time also provided information and fishery surveys which spurred my interest even further.

Fishing partners during some of my more formative years on spring ponds which helped me gather information include Dennis Van Oss, my brother, Robb, and Joe Salkowski. Those who have helped gather information over the last few years about fishing on spring ponds include Paul Zagata and Jeff Parks.

For their patience and guidance, I would like to thank John Walker, Hugh Foster, and Ted Schoenke. Also, I would like to thank Dave Estes for the time he took to discuss aquatic plants and benthic organisms.

For his innate art abilities, I would also like to thank Dan Hansen who has worked very hard at doing the free hand illustrations and drawings found in this book.

CONTENTS

The peaceful solitude of a spring pond in Vilas County.

CHAPTER

One

INTRODUCTION

The peaceful solitude of a spring pond shrouded by an early morning mist brings back fond memories of days spent afield fly fishing for native brook trout. Watching in the early morning dawn as the surface becomes enveloped with tiny dimples as the brookies start to feed is an invigorating feeling. With fly rod in hand, the first cast is sent out over the calm surface in anticipation of the first strike. Then a small dimple appears where the midge pattern had just landed a few seconds ago, and a brook trout is fast to the line. The brookie bulldogs deep but soon it appears near the surface shimmering and splendidly colored in the early light of day. Satisfaction is received as the colorful, little brookie is released back into its pristine environment.

Of the variety of trout waters available to anglers in Wisconsin, spring ponds offer an unequaled opportunity for the trout angler to enter this magical world of the native brook trout. Brook trout still thrive in fairly large numbers in these small, remote bodies of water. Due to a generous supply of spring ponds sprinkled throughout the state, Wisconsin is still one of the prime places in the United States to angle for native brook trout.

Most of Wisconsin spring ponds have never seen a hatchery truck. This is due in part to most spring ponds being somewhat remote in nature. Some of the spring ponds which were once planted have since developed wild brook trout populations consisting of lineage from native and stocked strains. Also, there are a few instances in which brown trout have migrated to spring ponds from connecting streams. These nonnative species somehow seem out of place, although a large specimen occasionally presents quite a battle when hooked on light equipment.

Spring ponds have not received a lot of publicity, except for a few articles appearing in regional outdoor magazines and research papers done by the Wisconsin Department of Natural Resources which many trout anglers have never seen. Moreover, there is a mystique or secretiveness about these small ponds. Those who frequent these hidden jewels do not readily dispense information about them. Hence there are trout anglers from within Wisconsin and from outside of the state that do not have the slightest idea of what a spring pond is or where to find them.

Over the past twenty years, I have been observing, researching, and trout fishing spring ponds throughout the state on both public and private lands. This has allowed me to develop quite an extensive list of spring ponds, both named and unnamed, as well as information pertaining to these ponds. It has been my pleasure to have been able to meet so many people from throughout the state and discuss matters pertaining to particular spring ponds. Whether it involved talking to other spring pond anglers or fishery technicians dredging

A dark brookie from a Vilas County spring pond.

spring ponds, all information acquired has been useful. Being able to observe several different types of spring ponds for many years have also helped me gain a considerable amount of knowledge about spring ponds. Of course, the experience necessary to be successful fishing different varieties of spring ponds comes from the many hours that I have spent on the water pursuing native brook trout across the state.

During my undergraduate years, I had the good fortune of being able to carry out research on trout waters and discuss fishery management aspects with a state fisheries manager. Many of these studies involved aquatic invertebrate populations and chemical analyses of water samples. Also, I was able to take part in fishery surveys which provided valuable information pertaining to trout populations. Furthermore, I was able to view fishery surveys which were done on trout waters in the past to see what changes had taken place over time. This research provided some of the impetus for studying spring ponds in greater depth. Therefore, it is hoped that the information provided in the following chapters of this book serve as a starting place for those anglers or naturalists interested in acquiring knowledge about spring ponds.

A beautiful day on Elvoy Spring Pond

CHAPTER

WISCONSIN SPRING PONDS

AN OVERVIEW OF
WISCONSIN SPRING PONDS

here are spring ponds located in
Wisconsin? Many trout anglers in the state
are quite familiar with Wisconsin's wide array of beautiful trout streams but have little knowledge about spring
ponds. Spring ponds, also known as spring holes or just
springs, are found wherever kettle holes reach below the
water table of moraines. Moraines are highly permeable
earth formed by the last glacier. A steady flow of ground
water through this permeable earth provides a constant
water source for spring ponds.

Generally, spring ponds are nestled in the wooded
headwaters of small trout streams. In fact, trout streams
often emanate from spring ponds or are fed by one or
more spring ponds. Most spring ponds are remote in
nature and, in some cases, nearly inaccessible. Many of
Wisconsin spring ponds are encircled by a landscape
consisting of a mix of swamp grass, tamarack, alder,

cedar, balsam, and birch. Therefore, spring ponds are usually not affected by the clearcutting of forest lands, farm runoff, nonpoint pollution, or urban sprawl, although there are a few spring ponds in the southern half of the state which have felt the effects of the latter three.

These miniature bodies of water, ranging from less than a half-acre to sometimes greater than 20 acres, are found from one end of the state to the other. The majority of Wisconsin spring ponds are found in the northern half of the state with the greatest density of ponds being located in the north central and northeastern parts of the state.

Langlade County, which is situated on a unique glacial formation in the northern part of the state, by far has more spring ponds than any other county. Langlade County alone boasts of having about 200 spring ponds. This is a large portion of the states' total number of spring ponds. All things being equal, some of the most productive spring ponds can be found in this county. Furthermore, most of the scientific and angling literature pertaining to spring ponds has emerged from the state lands in Langlade County.

There are numerous spring ponds on public land in the northern half of the state due to large federal, state, and county forest lands. Several of these ponds have been hydraulically dredged by the Wisconsin Department of Natural Resources (WDNR) and are quite productive. Many of these projects have been completed in cooperation with the United States Forest Service (USFS) and Trout Unlimited (TU).

Whereas many of the northern spring ponds are on public lands, most spring ponds in the southern half of the state are privately owned and much harder to gain access to. However, there are productive spring ponds in the southern half of the state, but spring pond anglers familiar with their whereabouts are secretive about them.

To try to estimate the number of spring ponds in Wisconsin would be an arduous task. There are many spring ponds which have been given names. However, there are still many more spring ponds which remain unnamed due to being small and remote. Bodies of water less than 20 acres in size have often been left unnamed. Also, many of the smallest spring ponds do not even show up on quadrangle(topographic) maps. Therefore, enumerating Wisconsin spring ponds is not very feasible.

FINDING SPRING PONDS

How do you find spring ponds? This is the question I am asked most often by fellow trout fishers. And why not, this is the starting place for the angler. There are reliable resources available to anyone that is searching for spring ponds. The resources to follow in this section will help you in your quest to locate spring ponds. Choose from one or more of these resources, then prepare yourself for a unique native trout fishing experience on one of the many spring ponds in Wisconsin.

One resource is the fishery manager in the area you wish to locate spring ponds. The area fish manager may have valuable fishery surveys on spring ponds you wish to try. Keep in mind that all state fishery surveys are public-record. Fisheries' surveys often show the number of trout by size class. Also, average length and biomass may be found in some surveys. However, make sure the survey is fairly recent, or the information could be invalid.

Another resource for finding spring ponds is a quadrangle map. These 7.5 minute series' quadrangle maps are produced by the United States Department of the Interior Geological Survey(USGS). Quadrangle maps can be purchased from the USGS, map companies, or outdoor specialty stores. The preferable scale is 1:24,000. Quadrangle maps produced to this scale allow you to get the big picture of the surrounding landscape. Unless you know of a spring pond or someone who can direct you to a spring pond, there is nothing more valuable than these maps in the search for spring ponds. Quadrangle maps show just about every land feature. In fact, you may be lucky enough to obtain a map that contains one or more spring ponds which are labeled.

Once you have located a spring pond on a map, then the process of finding your way to that pond begins. However, there are a couple of questions you need to answer before you venture forth. First, is the spring pond on public or private land? Secondly, are there viable routes to the pond?

If you are in doubt as to whether the land is a public domain, then check a county map or plat book. Most up to date versions will show which parcels of land are open to the public. Also, private lands designated as Forest Crop Land (FCL) must be left open for fishing and hunting. However, please check to see if the land is still under the FCL program before trespassing, because these lands may be removed from this designation at any time. Next, check the quadrangle map to see if there are any nearby roads. Possibly all that is needed is a short walk from your vehicle. This walk, in all likelihood, will be through a swampy area. Check the quadrangle map to see if any swamps are present in the area you wish to travel. Finally, check if there is a navigable stream that leads to the spring pond. If there is a stream visible on the map, then you will need to take a field trip and view the stream. There will be times when a one mile canoe trip is needed to reach a pond.

Planning and making a trip to a remote spring pond is often as rewarding as the trout fishing itself. However, precautions should be taken when making a trip into a remote spring pond. If you are taking a trip into the wild by yourself, let someone know exactly where you are headed. Also, if you are venturing over land for quite a distance, bring along a reliable compass and a fishing partner. Besides a fishing partner being a safeguard, you will be able to share the beautiful surroundings and trout fishing experience with someone else. Fishing for native brook trout on one of Wisconsin's remote spring ponds is a memorable experience worth sharing.

As another resource to the spring pond angler, there will be a diverse selection of spring ponds presented in Chapter 7 of this book. This sample of spring ponds should be used as a starting point. After acquiring some experience on a few of these selected spring ponds, then search the extensive listing of named spring ponds in Chapter 8 and use some of the resources described above to find them. It is guaranteed, however, that the spring ponds you locate yourself will become the most cherished. If you find a spring pond which is remote, you may be one of the few to fish that particular pond during the season. This is because many trout fishers today seem to want to fish water that is well known and easily accessible. Remember that there is plenty of knowledge yet to be gained from trout fishing on spring ponds by those willing to put in the time and effort.

PHYSICAL CHARACTERISTICS OF SPRING PONDS

What physical characteristics do spring ponds have that are observable? Every spring pond has its own uniqueness. Spring ponds differ in contour, depth, and color. However, there are certain physical characteristics common among most spring ponds. Some of these characteristics are positively correlated with the productivity of the pond.

All spring ponds have a commonality of springs being the major water source. A constant inflow of spring seepage in essence defines spring ponds more than any other characteristic. This inflow of ground water will vary from pond to pond and season to season.

Besides a constant inflow of water, spring ponds also have a constant outflow of water. This constant exchange of water is important because it promotes proper oxygen levels and water temperatures preferred by brook trout and other organisms residing in spring ponds. Also, a constant exchange of water promotes the removal of organic materials from a pond. This in turn slows down a spring pond's rate of sedimentation.

Inlets are another water source for some spring ponds. However, inlets are not always noticeable. Many of Wisconsin spring ponds have one or two inlets, but they may be intermittent throughout the year. Generally speaking, when inlets are present, they are not a major water source for a spring pond. However, the presence of an inlet may be highly beneficial to the spring pond fishery.

Inlets, at times during the year, provide a recharging of new water to a spring pond and offer a protective home for young brook trout. There appears to be a relationship between inlets and brook trout less than 3 inches in length. Young brook trout can be seen holding in the slow current of an inlet intercepting microscopic zooplankton. Observing these small, native brook trout from an arm's length away is an interesting pastime. Here in the inlets, brook trout fry are free to feed without fear of predation from older year classes. Also, most inlets are heavily covered by alder which protects the fry from avian predators as well.

Obviously, a factor which will greatly determine the chances of a healthy population of brook trout in a spring pond is the amount of spawning area available. Most brook trout observed spawning in spring ponds used gravel or coarse sand. During fall and early winter, you can determine how large the spawning area is in a spring pond. This area will appear much lighter than the rest of the pond. This is due to brook trout fanning the gravel or sand free of all silt before spawning occurs.

Also, a large spawning area in a spring pond reduces the number of superimpositions of redds. A redd is a small, saucer shaped indentation the female brook trout makes for the laying of her eggs. This area is then covered over after the eggs are fertilized by the male. In spring ponds with very little spawning area, superimposition occurs when later spawning brook trout build redds over ones already formed.

One characteristic common among all spring ponds are outlets. Although there are variances in the size of spring pond outlets, for the most part, outlet streams are visible throughout the year. Outlet flow rates will generally vary from one pond to another. Also, outlet flow rates will experience seasonal variations as well.

Generally, an outlet with plenty of gravel and moderate flow is very beneficial especially when the connecting spring pond has limited spawning grounds. In spring ponds with limited spawning grounds, outlet streams often provide the necessary recruitment of brook trout to maintain a fishery.

Large outlets are much more difficult to obstruct than small outlets. For this reason, large outlets may have a decisive edge over smaller outlets. Damming of a spring pond, whether done by man or beaver, will obstruct the outlet flow and produce destructive results. Damming will increase the depth of the pond in the beginning but soon the rate of sedimentation will increase nullifying this effect. In time, the water temperature in the pond will increase and ground water inflow will decrease significantly.

The majority of spring ponds have lush weed beds. Nutrient rich ground water along with a mucky bottom provides the right ingredients for dense beds of Chara in spring ponds. Chara and other muck loving weeds thrive in spring ponds and often cover nearly the entire surface area of some spring ponds. An extremely large accumulation of Chara in a spring pond may produce a much faster rate of sedimentation. However, a certain amount of weed growth is important to the productivity of a spring pond.

Many aquatic invertebrates thrive in the dense weed beds of spring ponds and form a large part of the brook trout's diet. Also, the benthic organisms, which are the bottom dwellers, remain high on the trout's diet throughout the year. Therefore, the bottom substrate along with a lush weed growth provides a vital link to the productivity of a spring ponds' trout fishery.

Depth is perhaps the greatest factor in determining the carrying capacity of native trout populations in spring ponds. Spring ponds observed with depths less than 3 feet maximum appear to be limited as far as space available for resident trout. An eastern Wisconsin spring pond I visit frequently has problems with predation of the trout population by herons and kingfishers. This spring pond, which is normally shallow, suffers its largest casualties during low water conditions. In shallow spring ponds such as this one, it appears that avian predators may play a partial role in reducing the number of trout.

Fortunately, there is a valuable tool available for increasing the volume and depth of a shallow spring pond. As mentioned earlier in this book, several Wisconsin spring ponds have been hydraulically dredged by the WDNR. Hydraulically dredging a spring pond increases the surface area and volume without the deleterious effects caused by damming. The carrying capacity of the trout population may increase dramatically over time. Also, if the dredging process removes substrates which were blocking spring inflows, discharge of spring seepage into the pond may be increased.

However, along with the benefits of hydraulic dredging, WDNR studies have shown that there are some short term side effects. Due to the dredging process nearly wiping out the entire benthic community and aquatic plant life, there will be a shortfall in available food for the trout. The rate of growth in the trout population is often severely affected for a period of time. In some spring ponds, this effect has been very noticeable. All ponds, however, will vary as to the time it takes to adjust to the dredging process. Aquatic invertebrate populations in spring ponds which are not dredged entirely will bounce back at a quicker pace than those ponds which are dredged entirely. This is due to the unaltered part of the pond providing a starting ground for the recolonization of the benthic community. Therefore, the rate of growth for the trout in a partially dredged pond may not be affected as severely.

As you can see, there are many different facets which make up a spring pond system. All the parts of a system contribute to the whole productivity of the pond. If one part is disturbed, then the whole complexion of the pond changes. Therefore, it is of utmost importance to protect the entire area encompassing a spring pond system from man's encroachment.

DIFFERENT TYPES OF SPRING PONDS

Although spring ponds have certain features in common, there are striking differences among spring ponds as well. Spring ponds will vary in locales as well as nature. Here is an overview of three randomly selected spring ponds chosen from throughout the state.

Lying approximately a half mile below the Upper Michigan border, the first spring pond is unnamed and located on private lands. This spring pond is nestled in the middle of a floating bog which makes every step toward the pond a precarious one at best. At the edge of the pond, precautions need to be taken as the dark, tamarack stained water drops off too over a rod's length. This is nonwadable water to say the least.

This circular shaped pond is approximately one acre in size. As far as trout productivity is concerned, this spring pond would not rate high. It has a medium sized outlet at the southeast end which at times has been impounded by beavers. A small, nondescript inlet is present at the north end of the pond. Spawning areas are not visible. If natural reproduction occurs in the pond, then most likely spawning takes place over deeper springs which are not visible through the stained water.

The brook trout that inhabit this pond are extremely dark. Ponds which are tamarack stained often produce very dark brookies. In this spring pond, brook trout that are caught will range up to 13 inches. However, brook trout do not appear to be very numerous.

This type of spring pond is the most dangerous to negotiate and should be fished with a partner. A life vest is a must when investigating ponds of this variety. Commonsense should dictate whether the brook trout are worth the risk. Nevertheless, many spring pond anglers would hardly pass up a chance to cast on a wild spring pond such as this one.

The second pond to be discussed is found in the lowlands of a cedar swamp on public land in the north central part of the state. This irregularly shaped pond, with many undercuts along its shoreline, is fairly clear in color. However, during the summer, the weed growth is prolific, and the pond takes on a somewhat green coloring due to the bloom caused by algae. There is no visible inlet. On the west end of the pond, there is a sizeable outlet. This outlet has an ample amount of spawning gravel. Also, the pond itself has a major spawning area on the east shore.

The number of brook trout in this spring pond would surely rate among the best in the state. Brook trout can be caught from 3-12 inches in length, although the majority are quite small. The coloring of the trout in this spring pond varies according to size and where a trout is caught in the pond. Generally, the trout with the darkest coloring will come from the deep undercut shorelines.

The last spring pond to be discussed is located in the farm country of southern Wisconsin and has a very different set of characteristics. This spring pond is surrounded, for the most part, by cornfields. The walk to this spring pond is relatively easy. However, there is one point where a creek must be crossed. This area is full of downed trees and brush from a tornado a few years ago, but once traversed the rest of the trip is easy going along the edge of a field.

This spring pond is also nearly circular in shape. A large outlet on the southern end and a ditch flowing in on the east shore adds to the whole productivity of the pond. Unbelievably, this pond has very little aquatic plant growth considering the nutrient loading from the surrounding area. Also, very little brush surrounds this crystal clear pond. On a clear, calm day it is possible to see large upwellings of spring seepage in this relatively shallow pond. This constant renewal of spring seepage entering into the pond makes for ideal brook trout water.

The number of brook trout in this pond has varied over the last several years. Numbers were highest before the drought of the late 1980s. However, natural reproduction in the pond and stream is quite good. In this spring pond, brook trout have been caught from 4-14 inches in length. Quite a few of the brook trout are very colorful with orange and red undersides. When comparing the number and size of the brook trout in this spring pond to other southern Wisconsin spring ponds, this spring pond rates very high.

Beavers at work near the shore of a spring pond.

Hopefully, this overview of three very different types of spring ponds have given you an idea of just how diverse Wisconsin spring ponds can be. Obviously, there is a wide array of spring ponds for the trout angler to choose from. Therefore, it is best for the angler to try different types of spring ponds and gain experience and knowledge in a wide range of settings.

A colorful native brook trout

CHAPTER

Three

BROOK TROUT:
SALVELINUS FONTINALIS

HISTORY

*F*or a long time trout anglers have been fascinated with the brook trout. When the first white settlers and trappers set foot in Wisconsin, they found the states' creeks, rivers, and spring ponds teeming with these speckled jewels. In fact, brook trout were originally native to nearly every part of Wisconsin.

Although the original range of the brook trout in the United States extended westward to northeastern Iowa and Minnesota, Wisconsin was the only state in the Midwest so generously covered with brook trout waters. Even Michigan, now with all its renowned trout streams, was originally devoid of trout in the Lower Peninsula. In the land that would become Michigan, only the vast wilderness region now known as the Upper Peninsula of Michigan, which has no land connection with the Lower Peninsula, originally harbored native brook trout. Perhaps, it is the absence of a land connection between the Lower and Upper Peninsulas of Michigan which stopped the brook trout from invading all of Michigan.

Ichthyologists have conjectured that the ancestors of today's brook trout originally invaded the inland waters from the ocean and advanced southward ahead of the last glacial activity. It is believed that as the brook trout moved inland they entered the body of water now known as Lake Superior. Brook trout then spread southward to the inland waters of Wisconsin, Minnesota, Iowa, and the Upper Peninsula of Michigan. As waters receded and warmed, brook trout populations became established in coldwater habitats including the spring ponds of Wisconsin which are generally located in the remote headwaters of small trout streams.

GENERAL DESCRIPTION

The brook trout is the only species of trout native to Wisconsin spring ponds. In fact, the brook trout is not really a trout but actually a member of the char family. For members of the char family do not exhibit black spots but display light spots on a dark background.

Members of the char family are better known to the scientific community as the genus Salvelinus. The Latin name for brook trout is Salvelinus Fontinalis. In English, this roughly translates to "little char of the springs." A very fitting title for brook trout are never found very far from spring seepage.

The background coloration of a brook trout will vary according to what type of water a pond has or where in a pond a trout is found. Brook trout found in very dark, tamarack stained water or deep undercuts in a pond often take on an almost black background color. Those trout found in crystal clear spring ponds often have olive to grayish background colors.

All brook trout exhibit worm-like vermiculations on the back, dorsal fin, and tail. Brook trout have light yellowish spots mixed with red spots surrounded by purplish blue halos along the sides of their bodies.

Bellies of spring pond brook trout vary from white to orange. In some spring ponds brook trout only develop orange bellies during the spawning season, while in other spring ponds brook trout display orange bellies all year long. I tend to believe that this orange coloration of the belly is positively correlated with the diet of the trout in a given pond rather than the color of a pond. I have observed orange bellies all season long on both clear and dark colored ponds with high numbers of crustaceans. In particular, the brook trout in one crystal clear spring pond have some of the most brilliant orange bellies I have ever seen due to a large consumption of scuds.

Rounding off the color scheme of the brook trout are the lower fins which are tinged with orange and then bordered in black and trimmed in white. It is this white trimming of the fins and the ver- miculations on the back which easily identifies a brook trout when viewing it from above. The brook trout with its gaudy mixture of colors is one of God's most beautiful creations.

DIET

The diet of brook trout found in spring ponds will vary accord- ing to the food organisms present in a given pond. In the next chap- ter, food organisms found in spring ponds will be discussed. However, at this time it will be made mentioned that Chironimid or midge larvae, pupae, and adults generally provide the principal food source for spring pond trout. In fact, I have never seen a spring pond without a healthy midge population.

Freshwater shrimp or scuds are the next most important food items consumed by spring pond brook trout. In some spring ponds, I have found scuds to be in greater quantities than midges in the stomachs of adult brook trout. As mentioned above, the belly col- oration of brook trout found in spring ponds with large numbers of scuds will generally be somewhat on the orange side. The red or orange coloring of the flesh of a brook trout is also highly correlated with the amount of scuds it ingests.

Other food items that brook trout consume are dependent on availability. The following food organisms that can be found in spring ponds across the state include sowbugs, water boatmen, snails, caddisflies, mayflies, leeches, tadpoles, clams, aquatic water worms, and minnows such as sticklebacks, blacknose dace, chubs, and sculpins.

SPAWNING

As fall approaches, the coloring of a spawning brook trout becomes much more vivid. In particular, the male brook trout becomes a kaleidoscope of colors and develops a small kype on the lower jaw. Females also develop a splendid coloring but not to the same degree as her male counterpart.

Most spring pond brook trout are ready to spawn after one year of life. However, a small percent of the male population may become fertile the first fall of their lives. It is this early sexual maturity which makes this species very fecund and often leads to overpopulation and stunting of brook trout found in spring ponds with large spawning areas.

Most spring pond trout spawn from the end of October through December, although I have witnessed brook trout spawning in a small spring pond throughout the first half of January. Brook trout will tend to spawn in spring ponds over gravel or coarse sand with plenty of spring seepage in the vicinity. When a spring pond lacks adequate spawning grounds, brook trout will spawn in the outlet provided there is a gravel bottom present. There are times when brook trout will also spawn in an inlet. However, a steady flow of spring water and a gravel bottom are generally required for brook trout to use an inlet for spawning purposes.

The number of eggs laid will vary according to the size and age of the female trout. The smallest females may only lay a few hundred eggs, while a three-year-old female may lay more than a thousand eggs. Survival of fertilized brook trout eggs to the alevin stage is excellent in spring ponds as the eggs are constantly incubated and cleared of sediments by spring inflows. Brook trout eggs in spring ponds do not face the same hazards that their stream counterparts do. Eggs deposited in streams often have to contend with sediments covering them, scouring of the stream bed, and shelf ice forming during very hard winters.

This brook trout had been feeding heavily on snails.

SURVIVAL

Although the survival rate of a fertilized egg to the alevin stage is quite high, the survival rate from the small fry stage to an adult becomes slimmer as a trout ages. There are many perils which await the growing brook trout.

As the small fry free themselves from the gravel, they instantly become food for adult trout and other fish, if present, and large aquatic insects. Although adult trout do occasionally consume small brook trout, they are generally not high on the adult brook trout's diet. However, when other adult fish species are present, they may consume young brook trout. Large aquatic insects also have been known to grab a small fry unexpectedly for a meal.

In spring ponds with liberal minimum size limits, angling plays the biggest role in reducing the number of adult brook trout present. When spring ponds have no size limit, anglers may take trout from any year class. With a 7-inch size limit, most trout taken will be two years of age or older. However, the problem that arises on spring ponds with size limits of 7 inches or greater is that many small trout are deeply hooked by bait fishers and some will eventually die. Therefore, it should be stressed that artificial lures are best suited to spring ponds with size limits, so brook trout can be released immediately with little harm done.

Besides anglers reducing the trout population, avian predators often take a toll on the trout population. This is especially true of spring ponds that lack sufficient depth. I have watched blue herons and kingfishers for long periods of time on a couple of shallow spring ponds. They are somewhat proficient at catching spring pond trout. However, I am sure that the number of trout these birds extract from a spring pond are never as great as the number of trout taken by the angling community.

Heavy weed growth like this on an eastern Wisconsin spring pond provides a home for many aquatic invertebrates

CHAPTER

SPRING POND FOOD SOURCES

$\mathcal{S}$ pring pond anglers should make sure they get to know the types of food sources that are found in spring ponds. Some spring ponds support a diverse forage base for trout to feed on, while there are others which have a limited forage base. Therefore, the more knowledge an angler can acquire about food sources present in the spring ponds the angler wishes to fish, then the greater the chances are that the angler will be able to present the proper imitation.

The food sources that are found in spring ponds are dependent upon several factors. Those factors which influence the presence of certain food sources in spring ponds include water temperature, weed growth, woody debris, rocks or stones, and bottom substrates. Dense weed beds, woody debris, and stones are home to many types of aquatic invertebrates. Also, bottom substrates ranging from sand to muck will often determine which invertebrates will be present in a particular section of a spring pond. Water temperature throughout a spring pond will not only determine what type of aquatic insects and crustaceans will be present but also what type of fish will be present in a pond.

MIDGES(CHRONIMIDS)

Midges or chironimids are of the order Diptera and are the principal food source for brook trout in the majority of Wisconsin spring ponds. Often on spring ponds, the angler will see brook trout feeding on the surface but may not see anything in particular that the trout are feeding on. However, if the angler looks closely, minute insects can generally be seen swarming just above the surface of the pond. The small size of an adult midge is usually enough for the angler to determine its identity as there are generally no other flying insects in the vicinity of spring ponds which are this small.

Once the ice goes out on spring ponds around the state, midges will begin to hatch. In fact, midges can be seen hatching throughout the entire open water season. Different midge species hatch at different times of the day. However, some of the largest concentrations of midge hatches come off during the early morning and evening hours depending on water temperature and weather conditions.

Midge larvae are usually about 1/4-inch in length but some species may grow to 1/2-inch in length. Midge larvae are often called bloodworms at this stage. This name has come about because of the red coloring of some midge species. However, midges may range in color from black to white with many different color variations in between.

Generally, midge larvae are found in extremely large numbers in spring ponds due to large areas of the bottom being covered with muck and silt. The larvae of some midge species burrow into the muck, while other species can be found in dense numbers in weeds growing over mucky bottoms.

Once a midge larva has been transformed into a pupa, it is ready to leave its burrow and characteristics common to an adult midge are now evident. As the pupa ascends toward the surface, it becomes a valuable food source for the watchful brook trout. While a pupa hangs on the surface of a pond and wiggles to free itself from its skin, it becomes very vulnerable to feeding trout.

When a pupa hatches out into an adult, it rides the surface of the pond waiting for its wings to dry. In some spring ponds, trout feed heavily on newly hatched midges and can often be seen leaping out of the water after these small insects as they dry their wings for a few seconds before taking flight. Trout also ingest a large number of midges that get caught in the surface film and become stillborns.

Midge Larva

SCUDS

Scuds are generally second in importance only to midges as a food source to brook trout in spring ponds. However, in some spring ponds, scuds may be the principal food source for brook trout more than 6 inches in length where large numbers of these small crustaceans can be found. Scuds are of the order Amphipoda and, for the most part, are very prolific aquatic invertebrates. Coldwater habitats such as spring ponds with generous amounts of weed growth and decaying matter are preferred by scuds. By picking up a clump of weeds or decaying leaves and sticks along the shore of a spring pond, the angler can get a good idea of the number of scuds present.

Due to the scuds shrimp-like appearance, they have often been called freshwater shrimp. Scuds can grow as large as one-inch in length but most are usually half this size. Scuds found in spring ponds are commonly tan, olive, or gray in color.

Scuds are low light creatures and hide in weed beds and under stones or woody debris during the daylight hours. They become most active early and late in the day and on days which are overcast. When swimming about during these times of the day, the scud's body is straight and fully extended. Very often scuds can be seen swimming sideways. Thus, they are also known as sideswimmers.

For the most part, scuds are omnivorous with a preference for scavenging the bottom of spring ponds for dead plant and animal matter. For this reason, scuds are not only valuable as a food source for brook trout but are also very effective at cleaning the bottom of spring ponds.

Gammarus and Hyalella are the two most common species of scuds found in Wisconsin spring ponds. Gammarus are usually found in bottom areas which are comprised mostly of sand, although they may be found in other parts of a spring pond. They are the larger of the two species and for this reason may be more important as a food source for brook trout when found in large numbers. Hyalella are generally associated with decaying matter and softer bottom materials. Due to Hyalella's ability to adapt to different water conditions, they are more widely distributed than Gammarus which are quite sensitive to any changes in their environment. Nevertheless, wherever scuds are found in large numbers in spring ponds throughout Wisconsin, chunky, red-meated brook trout are also found.

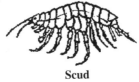

Scud

MINNOWS

Another important food source for adult brook trout in spring ponds is minnows. Brook trout greater than 9 inches in length commonly feed on minnows when present in a spring pond. I have found that it is quite common to find minnows that are three to four inches in length in stomach samples of large brookies.

The number and diversity of minnows present in a spring pond are often dependent upon water temperatures throughout the spring pond and spawning grounds available to brook trout. It appears that spring ponds with the coldest water and the largest spawning grounds available to brook trout have the smallest diversity of minnows. In other words, spring ponds with huge numbers of brook trout generally have smaller populations of minnows. For the most part, these types of spring ponds usually harbor only brook trout and brook stickleback.

Sticklebacks are small, spiny minnows which are often consumed by large brookies. Not only do stickleback minnows live in these icy cold spring ponds but they often thrive in these types of spring ponds if there are large beds of weeds. Sticklebacks will build nests out of weeds such as Chara for spawning purposes. An angler moving about the weed beds in the shallows of a spring pond will often disturb these small minnows. Sticklebacks when frightened will dart about in short, quick spurts.

Minnow populations in spring ponds with large areas of marginal trout water generally have large populations of undesirable minnows. This is often true of very large spring ponds or spring pond systems which have become filled in with thick, mucky bottoms that go on forever. In these types of spring ponds, unfavorable minnows such as dace, chubs, and shiners will take up residence in astronomical numbers. Spring ponds such as these and outlets associated with these ponds are often littered with minnow traps as minnow dealers ply these waters for the bountiful dace, chubs and shiners which enter these baited traps along with the occasional brook trout.

Dace Minnow

SNAILS

Snails are commonly found in spring ponds across Wisconsin and at times provide an easy food source for trout. Snails found in spring ponds are quite small compared to the snails most people are accustomed to seeing and measure only about 1/4-inch in length. They are usually brown, tan, or olive in color.

Snails do quite well in spring ponds because of the high calcium content present in these bodies of water. The large calcium content found in spring ponds is conducive to snails building solid shells. In particular, spring pond snails are quite fond of weeds such as Chara and Anacharis which leach calcium from the water and are found in these weeds in large numbers.

Although spring pond snails are quite small, they are most often found in the stomachs of larger brook trout. I have caught brook trout more than 9 inches in length on flies which have had their mouths crammed with snails.

Snails are very vulnerable as they migrate to the surface of the pond. As snails drift on the surface collecting oxygen, they become easy prey for spring pond brookies. Many anglers have been fooled by seeing brook trout which appear to be sipping insects from the surface, when in fact they are sipping snails right below the surface of the pond. In some of the clearer spring ponds, brook trout can also be seen rooting and stripping snails from weeds.

Snail

ZOOPLANKTON

Zooplankton are extremely minute aquatic organisms which are found in enormous quantities in nutrient rich waters such as spring ponds. The most common zooplankton ingested by brook trout are Daphnia. Also known as water fleas, Daphnia, are generally the largest zooplankton found in good numbers in spring ponds.

Although zooplankton are nearly invisible to the eye, they are a major food source for brook trout throughout the first year of life. Small brook trout can be seen holding in inlets and outlets feeding on tiny zooplankton drifting along in the current. If an angler looks closely, these minute specks can be seen riding along in the current if the water is clear enough.

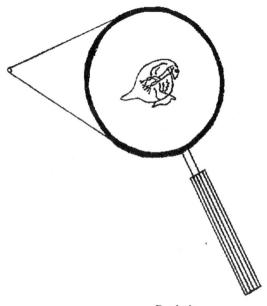

Daphnia

WATER BOATMEN

The water boatmen is a very common insect found in Wisconsin spring ponds. As you might have guessed, these little insects of the order Hemiptera look like a boat with oars extended outwards. Water boatmen can often be seen scurrying about in the shallows of a spring pond and occasionally ascending to the surface. The water boatmen makes frequent trips to the surface, because it needs to obtain oxygen. Due to its need for oxygen, the water boatmen is generally found in water with depths of no more than three or four feet.

The water boatmen also has a cousin which resembles it called the backswimmer. Differentiating between the two insects is quite simple when viewing them in the water, because the backswimmer as its name would suggest swims on its back. Both insects are brown in color with yellow and gray overtones with a light underside. Generally, these insects grow to no more than 1/2-inch in length.

Being that they must make frequent trips to the surface, water boatmen are very vulnerable to feeding trout. Also, during their mating season, water boatmen are easy prey. Water boatmen leave the water to mate and then return to the water to lay their eggs. It is during the boatmen's reentry to the pond that they are met by hungry trout. The angler that is fortunate enough to time the water boatmen's mating season in spring or fall will be pleasantly surprised to see trout eagerly feeding on these insects. I have only seen this happen twice and strictly by coincidence I might add. These occurrences took place once on a Forest County pond in spring and another time in fall on a Langlade County pond.

Water Boatmen

LEECHES

Leeches are generally associated with negative connotations such as sucking blood from humans. If the truth is known, very few leech species actually draw blood from humans. However, some leech species are actually used to siphon blood from humans in beneficial ways by the medical community.

Leeches are of the order Hirudinea and move about mostly in the dark. It is quite common to see leeches which are six inches in length but most are only a few inches long. For the most part, spring pond leeches take on a brown, olive, or black coloring with mottling present in some species. Color variations in leech populations are often due to the habitat they are found in and the types of species present.

In some spring ponds, leeches provide a valuable supplement to food items such as midges, scuds, and minnows but are generally not a principal food source. Leeches are most often found in spring ponds which are shallow and dark and contain large areas of muck. These are the types of spring ponds that the angler should pay attention to when choosing to imitate leeches.

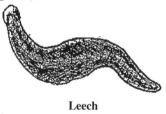

Leech

CADDISFLIES

Although caddisflies are not common to all spring ponds, they are found in good numbers in ponds with rocks, stones, and woody debris. For the most part, caddis which build their cases out of sand, gravel, and sticks are the most common species found in spring ponds and outlets or inlets connected to spring ponds with generous supplies of these materials.

Caddisflies are best suited to waters which are somewhat shallow in depth and have stable water levels. Being that spring ponds and spring pond outlets do not fluctuate very much in depth throughout the year, caddisflies have adapted well to many spring pond systems.

As mentioned above, most caddis larvae found in spring ponds are generally casebuilders. As larvae continue to grow during this stage of life, they often grow too large for their cases. When this happens, larvae usually discard the old case and build a new one.

Caddisflies also make a transformation from the larval stage to the pupal stage during their life cycle. This pupal stage will last for varying lengths of time with some lasting a couple of weeks. During this period of transformation, caddisflies seal themselves in their cases. Adult characteristics also become quite noticeable at this time.

As emergence draws near, casebuilding caddis can be seen migrating to very shallow areas of a spring pond. An angler that frequently visits a spring pond with a healthy caddis population may be able to time this migration and follow the emergence of these insects along with their mating flight.

Caddis usually emerge and hatch out during evening hours and overcast days on spring ponds. They will generally fly to brushy shorelines and remain there in these cool, shaded areas until mating takes place. This rest period may last for a couple of weeks. After mating does take place, females can be seen laying eggs over the surface of the spring pond or actually diving below the surface to deposit the eggs. During the egg laying period, caddisflies are very vulnerable to trout which have been activated into a feeding frenzy due to the massive numbers of caddis present.

Caddis Larva

MAYFLIES

Although mayflies are not always found in spring ponds, there are some spring ponds which contain populations of the giant Hexagenia Mayfly. Most spring ponds which contain populations of Hexagenia Mayflies are found in central and north central Wisconsin.

The nymph of the Hexagenia Mayfly burrows into silty areas of spring ponds. Occasionally, Hex nymphs leave their burrows during periods of darkness in search of food. Also, shortly before emergence Hex nymphs come out of their burrows for greater lengths of time.

Most Hex hatches take place in late June and early July in Wisconsin spring ponds. During this time period, Hex nymphs begin to emerge under the cover of darkness shortly after dusk. Hexagenia nymphs are strong swimmers and swim in a hinge-like manner toward the surface.

As the nymph reaches the surface, it splits its shuck and emerges on the surface as a dun. While duns dry their wings on the surface of the pond before taking flight, they are readily consumed by trout which have been feeding greedily on the ascending nymphs.

When the duns wings are dry enough for flight, they fly off to brush near the shoreline of the pond for up to a few days depending on weather conditions. They now shed their outer skins and become spinners. At this point they are now ready to mate. Once mating takes place, females fly over the surface of the pond and lay their eggs. Female mayflies then fall spent on the surface of the pond and are consumed in large quantities by gluttonous trout.

Hexagenia Mayfly Nymph

CLAMS

When found in spring ponds, clams do provide a supplementary food source much like snails do. Although clams may not rate high as something an angler may wish to imitate, it should be made known that they are often found in the stomachs of spring pond brookies.

Most clams found in spring ponds rarely exceed 3/4-inch in length and are most often consumed by adult brook trout which crop them off the bottom. For the most part, spring pond clams are found over mucky areas in a spring pond. Inventive anglers that wish to imitate these small clams should keep this in mind when making their presentations.

Clam

OTHER FOOD SOURCES

Although the ten food sources presented above represent some of the most common food items found in the stomachs of spring pond trout, there are other food items which are also consumed by trout living in spring ponds. Other food items include tadpoles, water beetles, sow bugs, tubificids(aquatic water worms), and terrestrial insects.

In the shallow portions of some spring ponds in Wisconsin, tadpoles can be found in large numbers in late spring and early summer. Most of these tadpoles are very tiny and measure between 1/4-

inch and 1/2-inch in length. Generally, masses of these small tadpoles can be seen swarming over sandy bottoms of spring ponds.

Some spring ponds have populations of water beetles which vary greatly in size. However, smaller varieties of water beetles seem to be consumed much more readily than their larger relatives. Water beetles can be seen at times moving around in the shallows of spring ponds but not in the same numbers as the water boatmen.

Sow bugs are interesting little creatures which are found most often in areas of decaying matter. The angler generally will not see these creatures, unless they pick up some decaying matter or stone. Personally, I have not found sow bugs very often in the stomachs of spring pond brookies, even though they exist in large numbers in many Wisconsin spring ponds.

Tubificids are the worms of the water world. They vary in color depending on the species and the habitat in which they are found. Most tubificids are fed upon by smaller brook trout, but they do provide an occasional food source for larger trout.

The most common terrestrial ingested by spring pond trout is the flying ant. These terrestrial insects hatch out in large numbers during late summer and are often blown by heavy winds onto the surface of spring ponds where they sometimes congregate in large numbers. The opportunistic trout are more than happy to see them appear on the surface of the pond and do feed ravenously on these unfortunate insects when they are present.

Stones and weeds in an outlet provide a place of refuge for many invertebrates

A light canoe can be a valuable piece of equipment for spring pond fishing

CHAPTER

TACKLE AND EQUIPMENT

*T*he tackle that a trout angler chooses to use is a matter of preference. However, when an angler enters the world of spring pond fishing, the tackle an angler uses will need to be refined. This is because the spring pond angler will often be fishing on small, clear waters for skittish trout where every cast counts.

Native brook trout in spring ponds are very wary. They have evolved this way for thousands of years to survive. Watching every movement overhead for feathery predators is an instinct built into native trout in spring ponds and, for that matter, trout that have become wild as well. Therefore, the approach an angler takes must be one of stealth and patience. Along with a cautious approach to a spring pond, the tackle used by an angler must be scaled down to fit the surroundings of these small bodies of water. Keeping these thoughts in mind, let us look at some of the tackle requirements necessary for being successful when fishing for spring pond brookies.

FLY FISHING TACKLE

The angler will want to choose fly fishing tackle that is on the delicate side when fishing on the majority of Wisconsin spring ponds. For the most part, the angler will be fishing for native brook trout in a small pond enclosed by a canopy of trees and brush. Therefore, precision and delicacy are needed in the fly rod that an angler chooses.

Preferably, the fly rod that an angler chooses for spring pond fishing should be in the 6 1/2 to 8-foot range and match a 2, 3, or 4-weight line for delicacy and accuracy in these tight surroundings. Shorter fly rods are definitely a bonus when one is probing for trout along the edge of a brushy pond or when trying to carry a fly rod through a maze of alders.

In larger spring ponds where the angler can fish from a canoe or float tube, it is best to use a 3 or 4-weight rod that is in the 7 1/2 to 8-foot range. A longer fly rod with a heavier weighted line will punch out a longer and stronger cast in case a wind arises. However, due to most spring ponds being located in swampy lowlands, strong winds will generally not be a problem.

For fly fishing on spring ponds, the angler will only need a single action fly reel. The main purpose a fly reel serves when fly fishing on spring ponds is to hold the fly line. Due to the majority of spring pond trout being on the small side, the fly reel an angler uses will not be tested very often. This, however, does not mean that the fly reel should lack quality.

A fly reel can go through quite a bit of punishment throughout an entire season of backwoods fishing. Thus the reel a fly fisher chooses should be durable. Also, an angler should find a fly reel that will be properly balanced with the fly rod chosen. For all practical purposes, the fly reel chosen should be light. The angler does not want to use a heavyweight fly reel attached to a light fly rod. Fly casting all day long with this type of setup can be exhausting. I prefer a very light handcrafted fly reel which weighs approximately two-ounces. This is often matched with a 6 1/2- foot 3-weight fly rod. When casting in tight quarters, the precision and accuracy I can attain from this outfit cannot be overstated.

Due to most spring ponds being somewhat shallow, the fly line an angler uses should be of the floating variety. A double tapered, floating fly line will handle most situations that an angler will face on spring ponds. It is very seldom that an angler will need anything else besides a floating fly line to reach trout that are down deep in a spring pond. Also, an angler will generally be making short, delicate casts on most spring ponds. Therefore, an angler will find that a double tapered fly line will be a better choice than a weight forward line.

The leader is the lifeline to your fly. Hence the diameter and length of the leader used will often make or break your day of fishing on a spring pond. As mentioned earlier, spring ponds are generally clear which at times makes the approach an angler takes to a spring pond a difficult task. Therefore, to reduce the chances of your presentation being seen as a fraud by the trout, the leader or tippet material for most situations should be 7X or 8X. For the clearest and shallowest spring ponds, my preference is to use a 12-foot leader tapered to 2-pound test without tippet material added to the leader. I often cut back to a 9-foot leader tapered to 6X or 7X when fishing on a darker colored pond or on a rainy, overcast day.

When everything is said and done, the majority of fly fishers will agree that they are most interested in what fly to choose for a given situation. In the next chapter, I will discuss which tactics to use for catching spring pond brookies. Each tactic to be discussed will include proper fly selection and techniques to use. For now, however, our discussion will concentrate on which flies have shown a great deal of success when used on spring ponds.

When selecting flies, the fly fisher should try to imitate the aquatic invertebrate and fish life present in a spring pond. As mentioned earlier, aquatic invertebrate and fish life will vary from pond to pond and season to season. Therefore, an angler should carry a selection of flies which will cover the majority of invertebrate and fish life that brook trout prey upon in spring ponds.

Freshwater shrimp or scuds comprise a large part of a brook trout's diet in many spring ponds. When the trout are not feeding on the surface, some anglers I know prefer to probe the water with a Tan or Olive Scud in sizes 12 through 16. I generally prefer to use a weighted Gold Ribbed Hares Ear Nymph in sizes 10 through 16 tied somewhat streamline. The mix of gold ribbing and hares fur makes for a somewhat translucent looking fly which resembles a scud in swimming position. When it comes to choosing a fly for all seasons on spring ponds, there is no fly which I can honestly rank higher than a weighted Gold Ribbed Hares Ear Nymph. Universally this fly represents many types of insects in their nymphal stages of life.

Chironimids, as mentioned earlier, are better known to most anglers as midges. In their pupa and adult stages, midges will be of great interest to the fly fisher. Generally, the pupa and adult stages form the most important food source for brook trout in spring ponds throughout the entire year. A Griffith's Gnat in sizes 16 through 22 is an excellent match for representing an adult midge on the surface of a pond. A Chironimid Pupa pattern or a Brassie in sizes 16 through 24 will fill the ticket when trying to match the pupa stage of the midge fly.

Several varieties of case building caddisflies can be found in spring ponds and spring pond outlets. Thus fly patterns which imitate the pupa and adult stages of the caddisfly will be quite effective at times. When caddisflies are emerging in large numbers during the evening hours or on overcast days, a Gold Ribbed Hares Ear Nymph in sizes 10 through 16 works well for enticing brookies which are honed in on caddis pupae as do LaFontaine's Deep and Emergent Sparkle Pupa patterns in sizes 12 through 16. Also, an Elk Hair Caddis in sizes 12 through 16 will generally produce when the trout are feeding on adult caddis.

Spring ponds which have large areas of muck covering the bottom will often harbor a good supply of leeches. Leeches will vary in color from olive to black. Fly fishers will find that a Woolly Bugger in sizes 8 through 12 should be all that is needed to imitate spring pond leeches. Black, brown, or olive colored Woolly Buggers produce the best results.

Many spring ponds have large numbers of minnows. Minnow populations will often be higher in spring ponds which are marginal for trout. Therefore, it is best to fish minnow patterns on spring ponds which have sizeable populations of minnows. Fly patterns which imitate the types of minnows present in a spring pond always seem to work best. A Blacknose Dace Streamer in sizes 8 through 12 will imitate shiners, chubs, and mud minnows. When sculpins are present, use a Muddler Minnow in sizes 10 and 12. Stickleback minnows, as mentioned earlier, are quite common in many spring ponds. Therefore, an angler may want to develop a pattern which imitates this minnow. In a pinch, a Mickey Finn or a Royal Coachman Streamer will attract trout especially in darker waters.

Certain food sources are not always available all season long to spring pond trout but may provide a valuable food source for trout for a short period of time during the spring. Here are a couple of organisms which the fly fisher may wish to imitate during the early part of the season. Tadpoles are common in the shallows of many northern spring ponds during the first few weeks of the trout season. A Black Gnat tied somewhat plump on a size 14 hook is a good imitation of a tadpole as is a fly called the Tadpole, which will be mentioned later. Also, at this time of the year an angler should carry some patterns which imitate the water boatmen. In spring, these small aquatic insects are quite numerous in many spring ponds especially in shallow to medium depth water. Water boatmen patterns should be tied in sizes 10 through 14.

You may wonder why fly patterns which imitate mayflies have not been presented yet in this chapter. The answer is rather simple. Mayflies are not always found in spring ponds. However, it should be mentioned that some spring ponds have populations of Hexagenia mayflies which provide a valuable food source for spring pond trout and exciting action for the fly fisher during their hatch in late June and early July. The majority of the ponds that contain Hexagenia mayflies are located in the central part of the state. The fly angler should carry a few Hex patterns which imitate the nymph, dun, and spinner stages of this mayfly to be on the safe side.

For the most part, the flies that have been mentioned in this chapter will cover the majority of aquatic invertebrate and fish life that the angler will need to imitate when fishing spring ponds throughout the state. There may be those odd situations where the trout may not be interested in any of your offerings, but these are the challenges which face every fly fisher. Take on each challenge by studying the prey that the trout are feeding on and experiment with different patterns. You may eventually develop a fly pattern which is effective for catching spring pond brookies.

When traveling to a backwoods spring pond, it is best to keep all your equipment on the light side. This includes the fly fishing vest you choose and also what you carry in it. Vests will often come in many forms and sizes and serve different purposes. If my trip to a spring pond is a long one, I will wear a light mesh vest. A mesh vest is comfortable and will keep you cool during the hot days of summer. When it is possible to wade in a spring pond above my waist, which is seldom, I will wear a very light shorty vest. This is an excellent choice for keeping an angler's gear dry when wading in deep water. A shorty vest will also keep the angler cool during the summer.

Fly fishing tackle that the angler chooses to carry to a spring pond should be kept to a minimum. The fly fisher's vest should hold only tackle which is essential for spring pond fishing. The angler may wish to carry only the following items on spring pond trips: a selection of flies for spring ponds, an extra reel, 6X, 7X, and 8X leaders and/or tippet material, clippers, fly floatant, forceps, a small pliers, small split shot, a knife, a waterproof flashlight, a tape measure, and insect repellent. Essentially, this is really all you will need to take along in your vest. When I know a spring pond quite well and wish to travel lightly, I will carry along only a dozen flies, a couple of leaders, and clippers in my shirt pocket.

SPIN FISHING TACKLE

The spring pond angler that uses spinning gear will want to stay on the light side. There are several reasons for the spin fisher to use ultra light fishing tackle on spring ponds. First, when hiking to a spring pond, it is much more comfortable to travel light. Second, it is easier to carry an ultra light rod through the brush. Third, sporting qualities are enhanced with an ultra light setup. Finally, the angler will have a much better chance of catching spring pond brookies with ultra light tackle.

When the spin fisher is selecting a rod, it is best to choose one between 4 1/2 and 6-feet in length. Due to graphite being a very light material, a rod made of this material is preferable. Also, most graphite rods are quite flexible and will allow the angler to play a trout on very light line.

The smallest of ultra light reels is a perfect match for a light graphite rod. Ultra light reels should be filled with two-pound test line. Two-pound test line will generally handle most spring pond trout and will disguise the angler's offering better.

The type of spinning lure the angler chooses will depend on what the angler intends to imitate. Before the angler proceeds to fish, it might be helpful to know if a pond has a sizeable minnow or leech population. This is because spinning lures are often used to imitate minnows and leeches.

When the angler is imitating minnow life, the Mepps spinner has proven its worth over and over on spring ponds. The Mepps Company is located in the heart of Langlade County, and, as mentioned earlier, this county has the largest number of spring ponds in Wisconsin. The company's close proximity to so many spring ponds has made Mepps spinners a favorite among spring pond anglers in this area of the state. Mepps 00 spinners are an excellent choice for the spin fisher when casting for spring pond brookies. The angler should carry spinners in gold, brass, copper, and silver color. Pinching the barbs down or replacing the treble hooks with a single hook is a good idea because barbless and single hooks are easier to remove and will prevent injury to a brookie released back to a spring pond.

Another good imitator of minnow life is a very small Rapala in silver or gold color. The Rapala is a very realistic minnow imitation and its erratic movement entices many brookies to hit it.

A 1/64-ounce jig is a good imitation of a swimming leech. Generally, black is the best color to use when fishing for spring pond brookies, although it would be a good idea for the angler to experiment with different colors if a black jig doesn't produce.

The spin fisher should travel lightly when entering the back country. The angler that plans on spin fishing should scale down equipment needs to a selection of lures, an extra reel and line, a knife, clippers, insect repellent, a tape measure, and a waterproof flashlight.

WATERCRAFTS

As you now know, spring ponds will vary according to size, depth, type of shoreline, and type of bottom substrate. Therefore, if you choose to fish from some form of watercraft on a spring pond, then your choice will depend on these variables.

Spring ponds less than two-acres in size which have walkable shorelines are best fished from land or by wading slowly in the shallows of the pond when fishing from shore is not possible. Any type of watercraft on a relatively small spring pond will probably make too much commotion and scare the spots off of the trout in the pond.

When choosing a watercraft for fishing on spring ponds which are larger than two-acres and are not surrounded by a floating bog, my preference is a small fiberglass canoe or a light, one man craft called a Poke Boat. A small canoe or Poke Boat is preferable because watercrafts such as these are easier to navigate on a spring pond. A fiberglass canoe is a better choice than an aluminum canoe due to the noise that can be produced by a paddle or a piece of equipment hitting the side or bottom of an aluminum canoe. I try to stay away from putting a watercraft in on a spring pond surrounded by a floating bog, because it is too dangerous to try to attempt a launch or docking from these shorelines due to unstable footing. Moreover, these types of shorelines are generally open enough to make a reasonable cast, but please be sure to wear a life vest.

Generally, spring ponds are not deep bodies of water and often have large sections with mucky bottoms. Therefore, I am very hesitant to suggest that a spring pond angler fish from a float tube on a spring pond. It is generally much more difficult for an angler to get out of muck when sitting in a float tube than when wading. I once witnessed a fisherman in a float tube so embedded in the mucky bottom along a shoreline of a spring pond that I did not think he would be able to free himself. After flailing and struggling for awhile, he finally managed to free himself from the mucky shallows. Thus, before you attempt to put a float tube in on a spring pond, make sure the bottom material where you wish to float is stable and try to find a spring pond with some depth so your feet do not touch the bottom in mucky areas.

BOATING AND WADING EQUIPMENT

Depending on how long and difficult the trip to a spring pond will be, the angler will have to make some decisions as to what tackle and equipment to bring along. Equipment choices will also be dependent on what way an angler chooses to fish.

A remote spring pond

40

If you choose to fish from some form of watercraft such as a canoe, then by law a life vest must be brought along. As mentioned earlier, for safety purposes it is also a good idea to wear a life vest when walking along the edge of a spring pond that is surrounded by a floating bog. Preferably, if the trip in is not too far and you are fishing from a canoe or boat, it might be wise to bring a cushion along too.

There are a couple of other pieces of equipment I like to bring along when I am fishing from a canoe or boat. Being that you will not be paddling long distances for the most part or against large waves, I prefer short paddles because they take up less room and seldom get tangled up with other equipment or tackle. Also, I like to carry along a one-pound anchor with about 15 to 20 feet of rope attached so I can position the canoe for casting purposes. It is extremely difficult to maintain a position in the water and cast to a likely looking spot at the same time when fishing alone. Furthermore, a light anchor does not cause much commotion and is relatively easy to transport.

When wading spring ponds, it is best to wear chest waders. However, if you elect to wade in a spring pond with chest waders, be very careful where you wade. Most spring ponds have bottoms with muck that seem to go down forever if you step in the wrong spot. Unfortunately, if you are wading alone and sink in too deep, it may be tough to get out. Therefore, I highly suggest you take along a fishing partner if you choose to wade a pond.

MISCELLANEOUS EQUIPMENT

There are several pieces of equipment that will be found in this section which are valuable accessories for the spring pond angler. Some of these accessories should be carried on the angler the majority of the time, while others can be stored in the vehicle and brought out when needed.

The spring pond angler will at times face a horrendous number of torturous biting insects when fishing spring ponds during the warm, humid days of summer. There will inevitably be days when insect repellent just will not take care of these nuisances. Therefore, the angler may wish to invest in a bug jacket and hat made of fine mesh. When treated with insect repellent, a bug jacket will provide the angler with the greatest protection possible from biting insects. The angler will remain comfortable in one of these light mesh jackets while fishing for hours.

I consider polarized sunglasses a must when fishing spring ponds. Polarized sunglasses cut out glare on the water and allow the angler to follow the fly line. This is extremely important when trying to detect any movement in the tip of the fly line while fishing nymphs. Also, polarized sunglasses will allow the angler to see a very small dry fly lying on the surface of the water quite a distance away.

When fishing spring ponds, I do not feel that polarized sunglasses serve much of a purpose for spotting trout. If a trout is surface feeding, its position will be apparent. Otherwise, spring pond trout blend in with their surroundings and are very difficult to see even with polarized sunglasses. Generally, if you get so close to a spring pond trout that you can see it, the odds are good that the trout has seen you too.

Another important piece of equipment the angler should pack when making a spring pond trip is a light rain jacket. Rain jackets can be folded and tucked away in your vehicle and brought out when needed. Rain gear will definitely make those drizzly days much more comfortable.

Finally, when an angler is planning on spending quite a few hours on a spring pond, a canteen full of water is highly advisable. It is always a safe measure to carry water along when entering the back country during the summer as a guard against dehydration. Also, a high energy snack might not be a bad idea when spending several hours on a remote spring pond. A little extra energy on the hike out can't hurt.

When taking a spring pond trip that requires some traveling, you will want to keep the amount of tackle and equipment you bring along to a minimum and still feel comfortable with what you have chosen. No doubt choices will have to be made as to what tackle and equipment will really be necessary for the spring pond trip you have chosen. Be realistic with yourself as to how much equipment you can carry in when making a long trip to a spring pond. Remember you want to travel comfortably so that your spring pond fishing experience is relaxing and enjoyable.

Fishing spring pond brookies in cold weather

TACTICS

Which fishing tactic a spring pond angler chooses to use will be dependent on several variables. These variables will include but may not be limited to the time of year, water temperature, weather conditions, clarity of the water, and aquatic invertebrate, fish, and plant life present in a spring pond.

As the seasons change, the elements which affect spring pond fishing also change. Many of the aquatic invertebrates and plants found in spring ponds are affected by changes in water temperature. As the warmer days of summer approach, insect hatches on spring ponds become much more prolific. Dense beds of aquatic plants also become very noticeable on most of the spring ponds in Wisconsin as the fishing season progresses. By the middle of summer, many shallow spring ponds will be literally choked with aquatic plants such as Chara and Anacharis. Vast amounts of algae can be found clinging to these aquatic plants on the surfaces of these ponds.

As mentioned in Chapter 2, a healthy population of aquatic invertebrates coincides with lush weed beds in a spring pond. A large number of aquatic invertebrates often translates into an excellent rate of growth in the trout population. However, the problem which arises when spring ponds develop extremely large masses of aquatic plants is that fishing becomes impossible after early summer thus rendering all fishing tactics useless. Therefore, it is important for the angler to investigate and discover which spring ponds will actually be fishable all season long.

In this chapter, spring pond fishing tactics will be presented according to that part of the fishing season in which they are most effective. The seasons will be separated into the early season(opening day through the middle of May), late spring(late May through mid June), summer(late June through early September), and fall(latter half of September). Each season will be divided into a fly fishing section and a spin fishing section. Fly fishing tactics will be presented according to what type of aquatic food source is being discussed. Spin fishing tactics will be discussed according to what lure is being used. The variables mentioned above including the season in which the angler is fishing will often dictate which flies or lures to use and which techniques to incorporate. Keep in mind that some flies and lures are effective through more than one part of the fishing season as are certain techniques.

EARLY SEASON

During the early part of the trout fishing season, fishing can often be frustrating with the cold and windy weather conditions which prevail. Mixed in with these weather conditions are cold water temperatures which cause the trout to be somewhat lethargic and uncooperative at times. However, there are those magical days during the early season when brookies start to feed quite actively on aquatic invertebrates.

FLY FISHING

NYMPHS

During the early season, primarily around the opener, fishing the deeper parts of a spring pond can be quite effective. In fact, at this time of the year I like to probe the deeper parts of a spring pond with various nymph patterns while not necessarily imitating anything in particular.

Most of the spring ponds in Wisconsin have maximum depths of less than 10 feet. Therefore, as a rule, the majority of spring ponds can be fished in the deepest parts with a floating line. However, depending on the angler's preference and depth of a pond, a sink-tip line may be chosen in place of a floating line. When fishing the deepest spring ponds, a sink-tip line will deliver the fly to the bottom much quicker than a floating line but feel and control of the fly may be reduced. Hence the fly fisher should experiment on spring ponds with varying depths and choose the fly line that best fits each situation.

When fishing nymphs in deep water during the early season, remember to fish the fly very slowly. Trout at this time of the year can be very lethargic. Position yourself just off of a dropoff and cast the nymph, preferably a size 10 or 12, into the deepest water. Then let the nymph sink to the bottom of the pond and very slowly retrieve the fly by drawing line in or by using a hand-twist retrieve. Once you have a rod's length of fly line still out, lift the rod slowly and impart a slight twitch. This will often produce a quick hit. On the clearer spring ponds, you will often see brookies dart out of the depths to take the fly as it ascends towards the surface. The lift and twitch technique will provide some of the most enjoyable fast action fly fishing on spring ponds at this time of year.

LEECHES

When fishing early in the season on spring ponds with sizeable leech populations, the fly fisher should cast a size 8 or 10 Woolly Bugger to the deepest parts of the pond or undercut banks. Allow the fly to sink to the bottom, then retrieve the fly by stripping in line very slowly. The fly fisher in effect will be mimicking the slow, undulating motions of a leech moving through the water. Early in the season, this technique can be deadly for large spring pond trout.

MIDGES

Once spring ponds become free of ice, midges will begin to hatch. With some spring ponds in the north becoming free of ice in April, it is not unusual to see sizeable midge hatches coming off on opening day. Midge hatches on spring ponds can cause early season feeding frenzies by brook trout which have been waiting out the long, hard winter under the ice.

After many years of experimenting on spring ponds with midge imitations, I have found imitations of the adult to be just as effective as pupa and larva imitations. Most stillwater fly fishing authorities, on the other hand, have generally found pupa imitations to be the most productive. I cannot argue with their regional observations, but on the majority of spring ponds across Wisconsin, especially in the far north, adult midge imitations are as productive as pupa and larva imitations. However, there will be days during the fishing season when one stage of midge life may prove to be more effective than another. Nevertheless, midges in any stage of life are usually found in stomach samples of brook trout in spring ponds and, for the most part, are the most vital food source for spring pond trout.

When spring pond brookies are feeding on adult midges, a size 18 Griffith's Gnat has proven its worth over and over again as an excellent producer. Brook trout even in the clearest spring ponds will take a Griffith's Gnat without much hesitation, although a size 22 may be needed. Another effective pattern when imitating adult midges is Kaufman's Chironimid Adult pattern. This pattern also imitates the blood thirsty adult mosquito rather nicely.

When fishing adult imitations at this time of year, it is best to allow the fly to just sit on the surface and be blown around naturally without any movement imparted by the angler. Remember that casting midge imitations over feeding trout is always more productive than casting over the water blindly.

There are two effective ways of presenting a midge pupa during the early season. The first method involves fishing over brookies which are resisting your adult imitation. Although these occurrences are seldom seen on spring ponds when brookies are feeding near or on the surface, they do happen occasionally. When they do occur, switch to a pupa imitation dabbed with a little fly floatant. The fly will lie in the surface film and will often entice brookies which are feeding on pupae in the surface film trying to shuck their cases or the cases themselves drifting on the surface.

The other method of presenting pupa imitations during the early season is to allow the fly to sink to the bottom. Let the fly sit for awhile once you believe it has reached the bottom, then very slowly make one foot strips of the line. After each strip of the line, let the fly sink a couple of seconds. Continue this pattern until there is about a rod's length of fly line out, then as with fishing other nymphs on a deep line slowly lift and twitch the rod at the same time.

It is preferable to use a 7 1/2 to 8-foot 3-weight fly rod with at least a 12 foot leader tapered to 7X or 8X when fishing these tiny imitations. The fly fisher will need to make soft, delicate casts which can best be accomplished with a light, delicate rod and a long, wispy leader.

The angler will find that overcast days produce some of the best results when midge fishing early in the season. Even during some incredibly cold, overcast days in the north, I have taken brookies on adult and pupa imitations. Once after a mile hike through slushy snow to one of Wisconsin's northern most spring ponds, I managed to catch and release a couple of brook trout on a size 18 Griffith's Gnat in a snowstorm. There have also been opening weekends in which the temperature has hovered around the 30 degree mark in the morning when brookies could be seen feeding sporadically on midges. On one of these opening weekends to my delight, I managed to catch and release 12 nice brook trout on a Griffith's Gnat without moving a step.

SPIN FISHING

JIGS

Spinning lures must be presented very slowly during the early season for the spin fisher to be successful. Generally, small spinners and jigs will produce the best results when fished in the deepest parts of a spring pond.

When jig fishing during the early season, the spin fisher should try a black, 1/64-ounce jig. Cast the jig out to the deepest parts of the pond and let it sink to the bottom. The jig should be brought to life by imparting a slow raising of the rod and then lowering of the rod while reeling in excess line. Much like the fly fisher imitating the swimming motions of a leech, the spin fisher will also achieve this movement with this jigging technique. Jigs have produced some very nice-sized trout during the early season. However, remember to reel in slowly, because large trout will not expend too much energy chasing a lure or fly at this time of year.

SPINNERS

A Mepps 00 spinner is an excellent choice at this time of year and can be used effectively by the spring pond angler. When using spinners, the angler should allow the lure to reach the bottom. Then the spinner should be brought in very slowly and steady. Spinners are an excellent imitator of minnow life and should be carried in a variety of colors including copper, gold, brass, and silver. Preferably, the angler should try to match the color of the spinner to be used with the color of the minnows present in a spring pond. If the angler is trying new water, then the angler will need to experiment with different colors until the appropriate one is found.

LATE SPRING

Generally, fishing during the latter part of spring produces the fastest action of the entire season. Forage minnows and aquatic invertebrates along with the angler's quarry, the spring pond brookie, have now come to life with warming water temperatures. Large numbers of invertebrates and minnows are found taking up residence in the lush weed beds which have now formed.

FLY FISHING

SCUDS

Stomach samples taken of spring pond brook trout have shown that they ingest large numbers of scuds at this time of year. In fact, when studying the number of food organisms found in the stomachs of brook trout in various spring ponds during this period, scuds often outnumbered midges. The angler should be aware of which spring ponds harbor large numbers of scuds when choosing flies and techniques to be used.

Scuds are low light creatures. They are very seldom seen out and about during daylight hours. Thus the angler when presenting scud imitations should keep this in mind. The best times to fish scud patterns are at dusk, at dawn, and during overcast days.

A Tan or Olive Scud pattern in sizes 12 through 16 works very well as does a weighted Gold Ribbed Hares Ear Nymph when imitating scuds. For best results, scud patterns should be fished during low light conditions in shallow portions of spring ponds where scuds are generally found. Preferably, scuds should be fished around some form of cover such as weed beds or logs. My preference is to cast among mazes of drown timber along the shoreline. Once the angler makes a cast and the fly hits the water, line should be drawn in immediately to avoid getting hung up. Brook trout will often dart out from under one of these logs and strike the fly immediately after it has entered the water. You may lose some flies fishing among the drown timbers, but the number of brook trout caught will generally outweigh the losses.

During heavy summer rains or thunderstorms, the action an angler can have when fly fishing with scuds can be electrifying. Please pardon the pun. I do not suggest that an angler should wave a graphite fly rod through the air while standing chest deep in the middle of a spring pond when lightning is striking all around. However, during thunderstorms which are accompanied by heavy rains, lunatics such as myself can attest to the fact that spring pond brookies go crazy over scuds. Some of these brookies can be quite large.

CADDISFLIES

During June, caddisflies will start to appear in large numbers. Often caddisfly hatches peak on spring ponds in the middle of June depending on which part of the state a pond is located. On calm evenings, you can often see brook trout in a feeding frenzy when large numbers of caddisflies are hatching. Brook trout during these feeding frenzies can be seen chasing and slashing after adult caddisflies which are trying to make their exit off the surface of the pond.

The angler at this time should be prepared with an assortment of caddisfly imitations. During the beginning stages of a hatch, a Deep Sparkle Pupa in sizes 10 through 16 can be very effective. The fly fisher should carry this fly in various colors, although brown and green are usually good choices. It is best to cast the fly out and allow it to sink to the bottom. Then the fly should be drawn in slowly. Most strikes occur when the fly starts its ascent. Some of these hits can be quite startling.

An Emergent Sparkle Pupa can be used to imitate caddis pupae as they try to free themselves from their shucks and the surface film. When using an Emergent Sparkle Pupa, the angler should fish the fly near the surface and impart a slight twitch every once in awhile. Many vicious strikes occur when using this particular fly and technique, so be prepared.

When brookies can be seen chasing, slurping, and slashing at adult caddisflies trying to take flight, the fly fisher should change tactics. I have found that an Elk Hair Caddis in sizes 10 through 16 can be a good imitation of an adult caddis at this time. When imitating an adult caddis, the angler can fish the fly still or occasionally skitter it across the surface.

Another fine adult caddis imitation is the Dancing Caddis.

When using this pattern, the angler will want to attempt to make the fly dance. A long, supple leader will make it easier to accomplish this task. Once the cast is laid out, the angler should raise the rod to a vertical position and then snap it down hard. This sends a rippling effect through the fly line and leader and in effect makes the fly dance. You may lose some flies using this technique due to hard strikes, but you may very well catch some very nice-sized trout.

MIDGES

Midge hatches intensify as the fishing season progresses into June. Hatches are greatest on overcast days or during the twilight hours. On some calm June evenings, midges and caddisflies can often be seen hatching at the same time. It is not uncommon even on small spring ponds to see these two insects hatching out over different parts of a pond. The larger trout will generally have a fix on the caddisflies, while the underlings will be midging if both insects are appearing in large numbers.

There are times, however, when the angler will be faced with a double hatch occurring in the same area of a pond. If this occurs, the fly fisher will need to examine the situation closely and do some experimenting with different flies to determine which insect is of greatest interest to the trout. These moments on the water can often lead to total frustration when the angler has no success while fishing over so many feeding trout during a double hatch. Please don't be discouraged by a fishless evening. There is always something to be learned from experiences such as these.

When just midges are hatching in large numbers, the angler will not have too many decisions to make. During the twilight hours at this time of year, I definitely prefer to use a dry fly. Once again, a size 18 Griffith's Gnat will fill the ticket when the brookies are midging on the surface. The angler may choose to skate the fly across the surface or fish it without any movement. For best results when fishing with adult midge imitations, the angler should use a long, fine leader.

TADPOLES

Due to the majority of Wisconsin spring ponds being surrounded by swampy lowlands, there are usually large populations of frogs in the vicinity of spring ponds. Thus large numbers of tadpoles can be found in the shallows of many northern Wisconsin spring ponds come late May and early June.

During this time period while the tadpoles are developing in the shallows, spring pond trout feed on them early and late in the day. Masses of tadpoles provide easy prey for spring pond trout being that they move slowly within these clusters. Therefore, trout can consume large quantities of tadpoles very quickly in one small area.

When imitating tadpoles, it is best to key in on ponds with substantial populations of tadpoles. In the clearer spring ponds with sandy or gravelly bottoms along the shoreline, the angler can easily locate tadpoles. Dark masses of tadpoles are highlighted over these light bottoms.

When imitating tadpoles, a plump Black Gnat on a size 14 hook can be effective. However, a fellow fly fisher and I like to imitate tadpoles with a simple fly we call the Tadpole. The Tadpole Fly looks like a black egg pattern tied with a small marabou tail. Generally, this fly is tied on a size 14 hook with a little weight, and eyes can be applied for aesthetic looks.

Try the Tadpole Fly early in the morning or around dusk when trout are on the prowl in the shallows of a pond. Work the fly very slowly with a pause now and then. Occasionally, the angler can impart a slight twitch to bring the fly to life.

WATER BOATMEN

The water boatmen and its slightly larger relative, the back-swimmer, are often found in large numbers in the shallower portions of spring ponds during spring. As mentioned earlier, the water boatmen is somewhat unique in that it must scurry around looking for food but also must come to the surface for oxygen. If the angler looks closely, water boatmen can be seen scurrying around in just inches of water. Occasionally, one will scoot to the surface for air and then descend again to the bottom. Because water boatmen must come to the surface, they are generally found in water no deeper than a few feet at the most. Unfortunately, the water boatmen's need to rise to the surface is often its undoing. For during the early morning and night time hours trout will devour them on their ascent towards the surface.

A pattern called the Boatmen Fly tied in sizes 10 through 14 can be effective during the early morning and around dusk. The angler should take advantage of the movements that the boatmen makes when presenting this fly. After the cast is made, allow the fly to sink to the bottom. The angler should then impart some erratic movements to the fly with a slight pause in between each movement. This should then be followed by a slow raising of the rod to simulate the ascent of the boatmen to the surface. The majority of the strikes will come during the ascent to the surface. However, be ready for a strike at any time.

MINNOWS

Minnows can often be found in spring ponds throughout the entire season. The numbers and types of minnows present in a spring pond often has to do with the quality of the pond. Generally, the coldest and purest spring ponds will have the least diversity of minnows. For the most part, these spring ponds will only support brook trout and stickleback minnows with an occasional population of dace and sculpins.

In spring ponds which have large sections with marginal water temperatures throughout most of the summer, large populations of minnows often take up residence. Other fish species such as chubs, shiners, and panfish often outnumber the trout by a large margin in these types of spring ponds. The trout, however, tend to grow rather fast and large in these ponds due to the enormous number of minnows present and the lack of competition with other trout. Spring ponds with large numbers of minnows are the best ponds to fish with bucktails and streamers.

A size 10 or 12 Blacknose Dace is an effective pattern when searching for spring pond trout, because it imitates several types of minnows quite nicely. Where the fly angler chooses to fish this minnow imitation will depend on the time of day.

During the early morning and evening hours, trout will prowl the shallower portions of a pond for minnows. This is often the best time to use minnow imitations. A Blacknose Dace can be worked through the shallows with short strips of the line. In between strips of the line, the angler should pause and let the fly rest for a few seconds. There is no need for the angler to make all kinds of wild, erratic movements with the rod when imitating minnows in spring ponds. In quiet settings such as the shallows of spring ponds, brook trout can be frightened very easily. Using the strip and pause method will prove to be much more effective for the fly fisher when presenting minnow imitations in the shallows of spring ponds.

When the fly angler is fishing minnow imitations in deep water, the fly should be allowed to sink to the bottom. In the deeper ponds as with fishing nymphs, the fly fisher may wish to use a sink-tip line. A good fly pattern to use in deep water is the Muddler Minnow. It is best to move the fly a few inches along the bottom and then let it rest awhile like a real sculpin. Work the fly in the entire way using this technique. One retrieve will take quite awhile, but be patient for in the long run you may entice some large trout.

MAYFLIES

Some spring ponds in Wisconsin, particularly those ponds in the central part of the state, contain thriving populations of the giant mayfly, Hexagenia Limbata. For the most part, it is one of the few mayflies found in spring ponds. In fact, many spring ponds are devoid of mayflies altogether.

The Hexagenia mayfly has been publicized widely in many books and articles. It is very common to hear about the tremendous hatches that occur in the sandy streams of central Wisconsin. It is the hatch of this mayfly which drives trout crazy as well as the fly fisher.

Generally, Hexagenia mayflies will hatch out at night in total darkness. Water temperature often plays a central part in determining when this will happen as do weather conditions. Therefore, where a spring pond is located in the state will play a major role. Hex hatches on most spring ponds will occur from the middle of June in the southern and central ponds to as late as the end of July on some northern spring ponds. The fly fisher should keep all of these facts in mind when planning a spring pond trip in search of a Hex hatch.

During the early part of the hatch when nymphs are emerging, it is a good idea to fish a Hex Nymph pattern or a Woolly Bugger on a deep line. There have been many Hex patterns developed for imitating the nymphal stage, but a Woolly Bugger with its marabou tail will simulate the movements of the Hex nymph rather nicely. Once the fly has reached bottom, the angler should retrieve the fly while twitching the rod. This gives the fly a real life look much like the undulating or hinge-like movements of the nymph. When the fly reaches the surface, the angler should swim it a little on the surface before trying a new cast.

When nymphs begin hatching out in earnest, it will now be dark. Many fly fishers make sure they have changed to a Hex dun pattern before complete darkness has fallen, so they are ready for the trout when they start surface feeding. A fly fisher fishing on a spring pond during the Hex hatch has a decisive advantage over one fishing on a stream, because the spring pond angler will generally have more casting room. This is especially true if the angler is fishing from a canoe on a larger pond.

Once darkness has fallen and trout start feeding on the surface, the angler should try to focus on individual trout if possible. Make casts to trout that are feeding nearby. At the sight or sound of a trout surfacing near the vicinity where your fly has fallen it is always best to strike gently. More often than not the angler will strike when nothing actually has hit the fly. However, sometimes this movement of the fly will illicit a vicious strike, even though there was no take originally. The length of this feeding frenzy on Hex duns can vary greatly. Hitting the hatch just right can be extremely exciting.

Once the duns leave the surface, they will fly to nearby shrubbery and shed their outer skin. Mayflies are known as spinners at this stage and are ready to mate. Depending on weather conditions, mayflies may wait up to a few days before shedding their outer skin. After mayflies mate, the female flies over the surface of the pond and deposits her eggs. Soon thereafter, the female will die and lie spent on the surface. The fly fisher that times this spinner fall just right can be in for some marvelous fishing with a spentwing mayfly pattern in sizes 6 through 10.

SPIN FISHING

SPINNERS

As the new year class of minnows and small trout begin to grow and move around, they become a valuable food source for hungry adult trout. By June, the new year class will generally be between 1-2 inches in length. These small fry are an excellent food source for the angler to imitate when fishing spring ponds at this time of year.

It is a good idea for the spin fisher to bring along an assortment of small spinners for spring pond fishing at this time of year. With the availability of so many small baitfish present during late spring, it would be wise to offer the trout a spinner which has a color that is similar to the baitfish being imitated. Also, keep in mind what type of baitfish you will be imitating when making your retrieve. Minnows such as the stickleback make short darting movements while chubs and shiners generally swim somewhat lazily unless frightened by a predator.

The spin fisher should use 2-pound test line and a very light spinning combination. Casts should be presented with the least amount of commotion for best results. Once again, fishing will generally pick up on drizzly, overcast days especially on the clearer spring ponds.

SUMMER

With the onset of summer, the angler will find that many spring ponds will be partially or fully covered with weed growth. Water levels may also be lower than earlier in the year. These two factors combine to make angling for these shy trout much more difficult. However, two constants still remain. Midges and scuds still provide the majority of feed for spring pond brookies.

FLY FISHING

MIDGES

As with other parts of the fishing season, midge hatches will continue throughout the summer. Midge hatches generally come off in the evening or during the early morning hours. It is at these times of the day that the fly angler will want to focus on when fishing midge patterns. In some spring ponds during the summer, midge hatches provide most of the fly fishing action.

While hatching on calm, humid evenings, midges have a difficult time breaking through the surface due to the thick viscosity of the surface water. Thus the fly fisher should imitate a struggling midge pupa with a Chironimid Pupa pattern fished with an occasional twitch near the surface. Remember that it is preferable to cast the fly to a spot where a trout has just surfaced. This approach often leads to a quick strike from a trout that is feeding heavily on midges. As mentioned, midge fishing can provide some of the best action when fly fishing for trout during the summer.

SCUDS

I have found that it is generally preferable for the fly fisher to fish with scuds during heavy rains in the summer much like in late spring. Heavy rains are a welcome relief from the sweltering heat, and brookies and scuds become quite active at these times. Scud patterns can be fished effectively among the openings in the weed beds and around logs. Due to the number of weeds present in many spring ponds during the summer, fly anglers will have to contend with removing weeds from their line and fly occasionally.

As water temperatures become marginal over parts of some larger spring ponds, the angler will have to locate spring areas. Deeper springs in some larger spring ponds can hold nearly the entire population of brook trout in a pond at this time of year. Fishing a scud pattern or other nymph patterns over these deep springs using the same techniques from early in the season can be quite effective.

CADDISFLIES

As summer progresses, caddisfly hatches start to taper off on many spring ponds. However, there are some sporadic hatches which will provide some quick action for the lucky fly fisher that is on the right pond at the right time. Use the techniques and flies that were presented in the late spring section.

SPIN FISHING

SPINNERS

When heavy weed growth sets in during the summer on many spring ponds, spinning lures have to be reeled in much quicker. There are some ponds, however, where these lures cannot be reeled

A nice brook trout stuffed with water boatmen

in fast enough without getting caught on weeds on nearly every cast. Therefore, it is of utmost importance that the spin fisher look for a pond without much weed growth or a pond with big enough openings in the weed beds to be able to make decent casts. As with spin fishing at other times of the fishing season, the angler should use the lightest line possible and make extremely soft casts.

FALL

Late September is one of the most exhilirating times during the fishing season to be on a spring pond especially in the northern part of the state. In the fall, the hardwoods and brook trout become a riot of colors. An artist could not attempt to do justice to a brook trout in its fall spawning colors.

Brook trout in the latter part of September tend to feed quite heavily on any type of unfortunate prey that crosses their path, although stomach samples would suggest that midges, scuds, and minnows still remain high on their diet. The appetite of a brook trout becomes quite voracious as it gets ready for the long, hard winter and the upcoming spawning season in late fall and early winter.

FLY FISHING

SCUDS

With the cooler days of late September creeping in, brook trout in larger spring ponds will start moving into spring areas with plenty of gravel and coarse sand where they will spawn in one or two months from now. In the smallest spring ponds, brook trout often live most of their lives right in the vicinity of spawning grounds if present in a pond. The ever present scud still provides a steady food source for spring pond trout throughout fall especially the scud species known as Gammarus which are fond of sandy bottoms. The fly angler may find that during the latter part of the fishing season brook trout will readily strike a Scud pattern during the daylight hours. This is very true of spring ponds with dark, tamarack stained water.

For the reason mentioned above, Scud patterns should be fished over spring areas with sandy bottoms for best results. The fly fisher can choose to allow the Scud to sink to the bottom before retrieving it or impart action to the fly right after it hits the surface. Trout will at times prefer to strike a Scud pattern when it makes its first movement off the bottom. Thus, once the fly reaches bottom, the angler should impart a quick foot long pull of the line to entice a trout into taking the fly.

At different times of the year I have fed brook trout a variety of aquatic invertebrates in a small spring pond where I can observe their movements. Invariably, brook trout will choose a scud over any other invertebrate presented to them at the same time. I presume the scud is chosen because it starts moving once it hits the water. Scuds have been matched against worthy opponents such as sowbugs, cased caddis larvae, uncased caddis larvae, midge larvae, and leeches with the same results. The scud is the winner hands down or should I say the loser after being devoured.

MIDGES

Although midge hatches become much more sporadic as the fishing season wanes, midge hatches are present nearly everyday there is open water. Brook trout are always aware of this fact as midges are their number one food source most of the year. The fly fisher would do well to try both pupa and adult midge patterns during September to see which one produces the best results. Techniques covered earlier in this chapter will continue to be productive. Once again, when imitating the midge pupa, use a size 18 or 20 Chironimid Pupa pattern. To imitate the adult midge, a size 18 Griffith's Gnat is a favorite.

MINNOWS

During late September, trout are always looking for a good sized meal, and this does not preclude feeding on minnows. In spring ponds with sizeable minnow populations, it is not uncommon to find minnows in stomach contents of trout caught in fall. One minnow alone provides several times more calories than a scud or midge pupa. Thus the angler may wish to wet the appetite of a large trout with a minnow imitation during the fall.

Minnow imitations such as a Blacknose Dace or Muddler Minnow when fished over spring areas may be just the right offering to entice a large trout at this time of year. Fish the fly slowly while imparting a slight twitch now and then.

An attractor fly like a Mickey Finn is also effective for a different reason. Because this fly displays a likeness to the gaudy colors found on the lower sides and belly of a brook trout in fall, brook trout most likely strike this fly out of aggression more than anything else. No matter what the reason may be for a brook trout striking this fly, the fact remains that the Mickey Finn produces in fall.

SPIN FISHING

SPINNERS

Playing on the same fact that spring pond trout take flies that imitate minnows in fall quite readily, the spin fisher should use a small spinner or other minnow lure to coax large trout into hitting. Preferably, the angler should try to match the color of the minnows present in a pond being fished. The angler should vary the speed of the retrieve until the right speed is found.

A healthy spring hole brookie

CHAPTER

Seven

A SELECTION OF
SPRING PONDS

*I*n this chapter, you will find information pertaining to several spring ponds on public lands in Wisconsin. Each of these spring ponds will be discussed in detail. The following information will be included for each spring pond: a map of the area for each spring pond(the top of each map points north), approximate depth and acreage, observations, a look at the fishery, tactics for catching spring pond trout, directions to each spring pond, and which quadrangle map each spring pond can be found on. This information is to be used as a starting point for those interested in acquiring experience fishing for native or wild brook trout in spring ponds. As mentioned earlier, after you try some of these selected ponds, expand your base of spring pond choices by using other resources listed in Chapter 2 or the spring pond listing in the next chapter.

Once you start fishing spring ponds, there are a few suggested guidelines. First, please remember that spring pond brookies are fragile, and deep hooking a brookie can be lethal. Therefore, it is best that you choose artificial lures with barbless hooks when fishing for spring pond brookies. Barbless lures reduce hooking mortality in brook trout released back into a pond. My preference is to use small, barbless flies. Small flies do not penetrate very deep and are easy to remove. However, many spring pond anglers choose spin fishing as their preference when fishing spring pond brookies. If you spin fish, please try to use lures such as spinners with the barbs pinched down. Generally, these lures can be extracted rather quickly. Secondly, handle brook trout as little as possible. It is best to revive them in the water. An angler may wish to use a light mesh net for landing trout while fishing from a canoe.

These guidelines are particularly important when fishing spring ponds with size limits of 8 or 9 inches or greater. In spring ponds with these minimum size limits, there are many small brookies that must be released. The handling of a hooked trout is of utmost importance. I once found five dead brook trout in the shallows of a spring pond. Apparently these small brookies were deeply hooked and left dead after a careless person ripped the hook out of them. This is a senseless waste of a precious resource. Therefore, please try to use commonsense when handling and releasing spring pond brookies.

There are also some guidelines to follow when traveling to spring ponds. Many spring ponds require a hike or a short canoe trip. Therefore, make sure you are in good physical condition before entering the wild back country. Also, some of the roads into these spring ponds are not improved, so precautions should be taken when driving on these two-tracks. Many roads have deep ruts and become quagmires in early spring, thus make sure your vehicle is equipped to handle these roads.

Keep in mind, spring pond angling is a unique and challenging experience and at times downright frustrating. If you don't succeed right away at catching spring pond brookies, stay with it, and be patient. Often it will take many spring pond outings before you become proficient at catching these speckled jewels.

MILLHOME SPRING POND

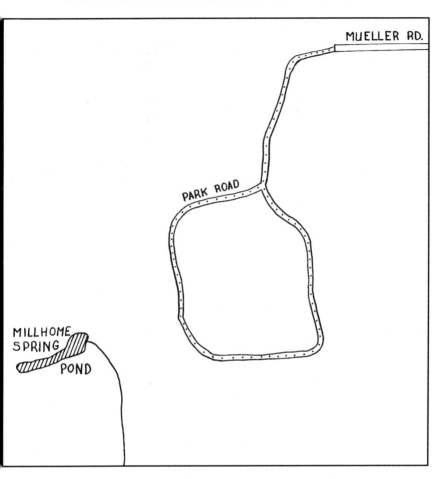

MANITOWOC COUNTY

AREA: 1/2 ACRE

MAXIMUM DEPTH: 4 FEET

OBSERVATIONS

Millhome Spring Pond is located on county land in the beautiful rolling hills of the northern kettle moraine. The land surrounding the pond is made up of evergreens, birch, and alders. At one time this parcel of land was used as a private trout hatchery. The remains of the well house can still be seen a short distance from the pond.

Millhome Spring Pond is one of the least secluded places in the state that still supports a population of wild brook trout.

Although this pond lacks size and depth, it does have a few features which make it somewhat productive. Millhome Spring Pond has a generous supply of spawning gravel in the middle and upper sections of the pond. Also, at the outlet area, there is a significant amount of gravel. Unfortunately, as I will mention later, the outlet has been dammed at times. If damming takes place from late November to early January, then the brook trout in the pond are cut off from that part of the spawning area available to them in the outlet. Not too far from the outlet is a spring inlet. The inlet runs all year long if the outlet remains open. This recharging of spring seepage from the inlet rejuvenates the lower section of the pond and provides a sanctuary for the young brook trout fry in the pond.

Hydraulic dredging took place in the pond in the late 1970s after the county purchased the land. Dredging increased the depth of the pond considerably. However, during the last fifteen years, there has been an attempt by some people to block the flow of the outlet. This attempt was to raise the depth of the pond even more. As mentioned in Chapter 2, blocking the flow of a spring pond outlet is detrimental to the health of the pond. Therefore, I have tried over the last several years to remove these obstructions but to no avail. This continual obstruction of the outlet in the long run has increased the rate of sedimentation to the point where the lower section needs to be dredged again. The growth of Chara in the pond is so extreme that nearly the entire surface area of the pond is covered by June.

FISHERY

There is a wild population of brook trout in Millhome Spring Pond. At the time the spring pond system was taken over as a hatchery operation it is believed to be the last native brook trout population left in Manitowoc County. It appears this trout population may still have remained native, even though it was used as a hatchery. The trout lineage that was there prior to the hatchery and during hatchery use were naturally reproduced. However, after the dredging of the pond took place, the pond was stocked with 500 brook trout, thus mixing with the native trout population already in existence. If purity tests were run on a sample of brook trout from this system, I believe a certain percentage may still show some native lineage.

There is a fairly large population of brook trout in Millhome Spring Pond considering its size and depth. However, due to the number of trout reproduced in the pond and the 9-inch size limit imposed by the state, the majority of the brook trout are quite small. Those who catch a trout of 9 inches or larger, of which there are few, will crop these from the population, thus leaving behind numerous small brook trout but very few large ones.

Although there are few large trout left in the pond, those brook trout between 5-8 inches in length produce plenty of offspring to sustain a wild fishery. Most brook trout will spawn in Millhome Spring Pond from late November to early January. In fact, the latest pair of spawning brook trout that I have ever observed building a redd in a spring pond took place one year in Millhome Spring Pond on January 13.

TACTICS

When fly fishing on this crystal clear spring pond, it is best to fish the first or last hour of the day or while it is raining. Some of my most productive fishing days on this pond have come during torrential downpours. It is almost an assurance that you will be skunked during the middle of the day when it is clear and calm. This is true of almost all spring ponds which are as clear as glass. Also, Millhome Spring Pond grows heavy with weeds, so try to fish the pond before early June.

Fly fishing a crystal clear spring pond in such small surroundings requires stealth and patience much like that required for spring creek fishing. Leaders should be long and fine. Sometimes this requires the use of 7X or 8X leaders. Try to use 1, 2, or 3 weight rods, because casting in these tight quarters requires delicacy and precision. Scuds, caddis, and midges are high on the brook trout's diet in Millhome Spring Pond. Therefore, try a Gold Ribbed Hares Ear Nymph in sizes 12-16, a Chironimid Pupa in sizes 14-20, or a Griffith's Gnat in sizes 18-22.

When spin fishing this small pond, try a Mepps 00 in brass or gold. These colors work best because the only forage minnows to simulate in the pond are stickleback minnows. Also, use 2-pound test line and make short, soft casts. Once again, limit your fishing hours to the early morning and the last light of day.

DIRECTIONS

Drive west of Kiel on Hwy. 32-57 and stay on Hwy. 32 when they split apart, travel until you reach South Cedar Lake Road, then turn left and travel to Mueller Road and turn left and drive into Walla-Hi County Park.

QUADRANGLE MAP: SCHOOL HILL

This spring pond does not show up on a quadrangle map but the outline of Millhome Creek does show up.

SPRINGMEADOW SPRING POND

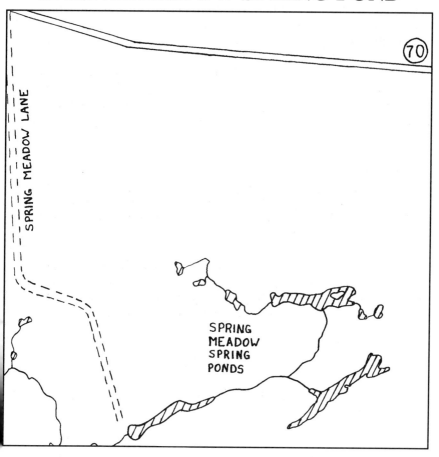

SPRING MEADOW LANE

70

SPRING
MEADOW
SPRING
PONDS

VILAS COUNTY

AREA: 4 ACRES

MAXIMUM DEPTH: 6 FEET

OBSERVATIONS

     The Springmeadow Spring Pond system is located in the Nicolet National Forest. The Springmeadow Spring Pond system is made up of three ponds split into two main spring ponds in the upper most part of the watershed and a flowage pond at the outlet. The spring ponds feed into the main channel which in turn forms the flowage. The area surrounding the flowage is mostly upland with a mix of evergreens and hardwoods. The two spring ponds sit primarily in a large marsh with the southern pond having uplands on the south shore. The water in this spring pond system is somewhart dark due to the number of tamaracks present along the shores of these ponds.

The flowage is studded with dead trees sticking out of the water and has the deepest water in this system due to the outlet being dammed many years ago. It also has the darkest water. The upper part of this pond along with most of the channel grows heavy with eel grass and lily pads.

The southern spring pond has its greatest depth in the middle. At the upper most part of this pond there is some spring seepage which is noticeable. This pond generally has a mucky bottom as does most of this system. Also, the upper section of this pond is quite shallow and has dense weed beds.

The spring pond to the north has some deep holes due to the water being backed up by an old beaver dam. Several old beaver huts are still present along the shores of this pond. There is also quite a bit of weed growth present but not to the same extent as the other spring pond.

FISHERY

This system of ponds has an average population of native brook trout which are very colorful. The southern spring pond seems to have a better population of trout than the other two ponds. However, the brookies that are taken from this pond are generally quite small. The middle section of the southern pond has been the most productive during the summer because it has the most openings in between the heavy patches of weeds. Brookies often hide along the undercuts and the edges of dense weed beds in this pond.

Occasionally, a brookie is caught in the channel above the flowage. Only once, however, was I successful at the outlet area, and this was on a very cold opening day. This area may get too warm during the summer for brook trout to tolerate. However, an angler may have success fishing the flowage and channel early in the season.

TACTICS

It is best to put a small canoe in at the outlet and paddle upstream. There may be a few logs to get over and deadfalls to dodge in the lower section but after you reach the channel it is generally clear except for the heavy growth of lily pads during the summer.

Due to the enormous number of midges hatching on a daily basis, I like to use a Chironimid Pupa pattern in sizes 14-20. Leaders should be long and fine when fly fishing in the shallower sections of this system. This is especially true of the upper section of the southern spring pond. Also, it might be wise to use a smaller midge pattern in this section. When fishing in the shallower parts of this system, it is best to try early or late in the day.

There is an extremely large minnow population in all of these ponds. Therefore, the spin fisher may wish to try a small spinner. Many spin fishers use small shiners, dace, or stickleback minnows. Early in the season, some anglers also use Hexagenia mayfly nymphs, also known as, wigglers.

DIRECTIONS

Drive east on Hwy. 70 out of Eagle River to Springmeadow Lane, then turn right and follow this bumpy, rutted road down to the lower pond. There is a lot of logging activity taking place along this road, so be careful.

QUADRANGLE MAP: ANVIL LAKE

GOODYEAR SPRING POND

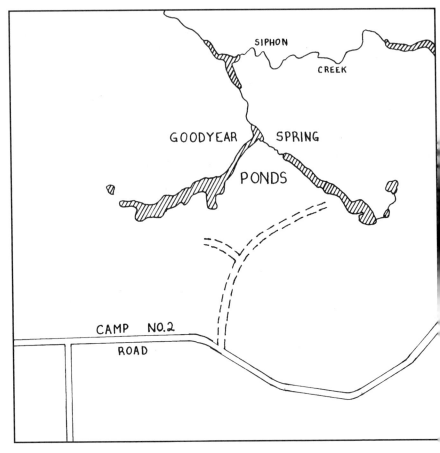

VILAS COUNTY

AREA: 10 ACRES

MAXIMUM DEPTH: 8 FEET

OBSERVATIONS

    The Goodyear Spring Pond system is made up of three ponds. However, only the two largest ponds will be discussed. The western most pond is the largest and has the greatest depth. This spring pond has been dredged and has a large spawning area. The water is very clear. The eastern pond is very much the opposite of the western pond. It has a very mucky bottom and is quite shallow with no spawning grounds. A small inlet, which originates from the third pond, enters at the southeast corner of this pond.

The outlets of the western and eastern ponds merge into one stream and then flows into Siphon Creek which is a slow moving creek with a small population of native brook trout. Another spring pond system called Siphon, which will be discussed later, is found approximately one-mile upstream from this junction.

FISHERY

The trout fishery in this system varies from good to average. The western pond is the most productive due to being dredged not that many years ago. As mentioned earlier, this spring pond has a large spawning area for the native brookies. This factor coupled with a decent average depth provides the right ingredients for a healthy trout population. Also, deep undercuts and a few logs provide cover for the resident trout. There is very little weed growth, however, in this pond.

The eastern pond is not very productive because it lacks spawning grounds and depth. This pond appears to have a much larger population of minnows than the western pond. An angler fishing the western pond may wish to enter the eastern pond from where the outlets come together. Also, an angler may want to canoe downstream and try part of Siphon Creek.

TACTICS

The western pond in the Goodyear system is no doubt the spring pond you will want to try first. It is best to fish this pond from a canoe. You can put a canoe in on the western end where the access road ends.

Midges as usual will provide interesting fly fishing early and late in the day. Remember to approach midging trout very slowly without making too much commotion. Try a Chironimid Pupa or a Griffith's Gnat. These two flies generally provide plenty of action when fishing over trout that are midging.

A size 12 Olive Scud is a good searching fly as is a Gold Ribbed Hares Ear Nymph. Work these flies around submerged logs and near deep undercuts for best results. Due to a large number of water boatmen present in these ponds, a size 14 Water Boatmen fly can also be effective at certain times of the year.

The spin fisher may wish to try a Mepps 00 spinner to imitate the minnow life present in these ponds especially the eastern pond. Work the spinner aroung logs, near deep undercuts, and the deepest parts of the western pond.

DIRECTIONS

Drive west of Star Lake until you reach Camp 2 Road, then follow this road approximately 5 miles to a "T" intersection. At this point turn right and drive a little over one-mile to a narrow logging road on your left which is not very easy to see at times. Follow this road all the way in while staying to the left. This will take you to the western pond. Right before the road veers to the left there is a logging road on the right side which will take you to the eastern pond. This is a very rough road to drive in on. Please obtain a quadrangle map of this area before attempting this trip!

QUADRANGLE MAP: STAR LAKE

SIPHON SPRING POND

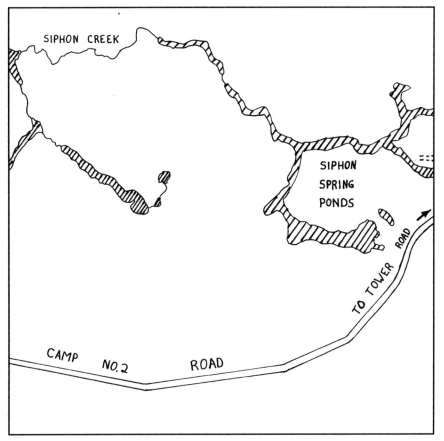

SIPHON CREEK

SIPHON SPRING PONDS

TO TOWER ROAD

CAMP NO. 2 ROAD

VILAS COUNTY

AREA: 9 ACRES

MAXIMUM DEPTH: 7 FEET

OBSERVATIONS

The Siphon Spring Pond system, which is the headwaters of Siphon Creek, is located in the Northern Highland-American Legion State Forest. The area surrounding this pond is swampy and somewhat remote and remains much like it was found by the turn of the century lumbermen. The Siphon Spring Pond system is a conglomeration of several spring ponds. However, the largest pond is generally referred to as Siphon Spring Pond and is the most productive.

The majority of the other spring ponds are quite shallow and mucky. The whole area is rich with spring seepage.

There are some uplands in the eastern area in which you enter, but the majority of the surrounding area is swampland. This area takes you into an era of days gone by. It is a very natural area, even though many years ago there was lumber activity in this region. It is still possible to view the remains of tracks left behind from the turn of the century timber operations. On the canoe trip in the angler will have to portage over these old logging tracks in at least one place, because the water level is quite low in this area due to the removal of beaver dams downstream. The remains of the old tracks can also be seen today crossing the largest spring pond.

FISHERY

Siphon Spring Pond contains a native brook trout population. The brookies of Siphon Spring Pond can be hard to catch at times. Although this spring pond is fairly remote, it does have a loyal following of anglers who know of its whereabouts. Most of these anglers fish with bait.

Due to the size of the pond, it is sometimes difficult to find strongholds of brookies. I like to fish around the old tracks, deep weed beds, and other woody debris jutting out from the shoreline. Brookies have been caught up to 14 inches. These brookies are not found in great numbers, but there are some nice trout present in this system. Natural reproduction appears to be adequate as there has never been any record of stocking of trout in this pond. Many of the smaller brookies are protected due to the 8-inch minimum size limit.

TACTICS

It is best to put a canoe in at the upper ponds and paddle downstream. The area where you put in at is very mucky. Therefore, be particularly careful where you step or you may sink in rather quickly and need some help getting out. At the pond you put in at, paddle downstream until you reach a feeder stream on the left side. Canoe up the feeder, which is the outlet of Siphon Spring Pond, until you enter the largest pond.

As mentioned earlier, most anglers use bait such as minnows, worms, or wigglers. It is in your favor to use artificial lures for these brookies are very uneducated. The fly fisher will want to stay with a 6X or 7X leader due to the clarity of the water. Try a Gold Ribbed

Hares Ear Nymph or any scud pattern in sizes 12-16. Also, give a Griffith's Gnat or a Chironimid Pupa pattern a try if you notice the brookies are midging. Once again, the best action is early or late in the day. However, unless you make camp or know the area well enough, I would not suggest fishing until dark in this area. It takes awhile to canoe back to the site you entered from. Also, there are several ponds to negotiate which could confuse the novice and get a person lost.

There is a sizeable population of dace, shiners, and chubs in this spring pond. Therefore, the spin fisher may want to try a Mepps 00 or 0 spinner in brass, copper, or gold coloring. Small Rapalas may work well too. Try different depths, but watch out for snags.

DIRECTIONS

Follow the same directions as described for Goodyear Spring Pond but instead of turning onto the logging road continue a couple miles to a "T" intersection. Turn left on Tower Lake Road, which is not marked, and drive slowly for about a quarter-mile while looking for a logging road on the left. It is best to park and carry your canoe down this unmarked road to the pond. Please obtain a quadrangle map of the area before attempting this trip!

QUADRANGLE MAP: STAR LAKE

ELVOY SPRING POND

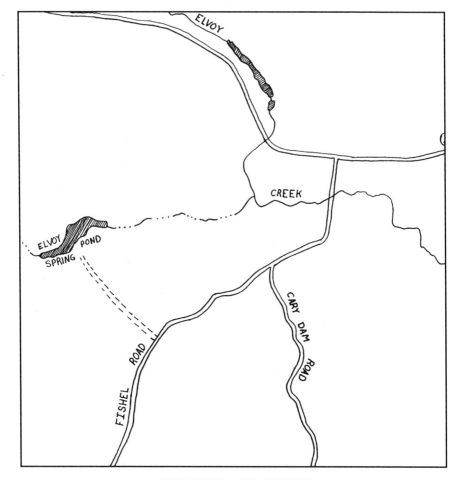

FOREST COUNTY

AREA: 3 ACRES

MAXIMUM DEPTH: 8 FEET

OBSERVATIONS

    Elvoy Spring Pond is part of the Elvoy Creek System and is located in the northern part of the Nicolet National Forest. Elvoy Creek is primarily a Class 1 trout stream containing populations of both brook and brown trout. The pond connects to the creek through an outlet on the northeast end. At times this outlet has been blocked by beavers. The bottom substrates of the pond are composed mostly of sand and muck with gravel and stones interspersed in a few places. On the southeast end is a small, intermittent inlet with plenty of spring seepage in the vicinity where the inlet enters. At the southern tip of the pond there are deep undercuts. A person fishing along the edge on this end of the pond needs to watch their step.

Elvoy Spring Pond was hydraulically dredged in the late 1980s. Dredging took place right before a couple of years of drought occurred. Trout fishing was closed for one year, and the next year the fishing season was open to catch and release fishing only with artificial lures. It took the pond a few years to recover fully from the dredging process and the drought.

The pond is surrounded by marsh grass mixed with alders and pines. The water is very clear most of the time, although heavy weed growth during the summer causes the water to take on a green coloring. Considering that the pond was dredged not that many years ago, the weeds have grown back in great quantity.

A boardwalk was constructed on the east side of the pond after dredging was completed. It is possible to fish off this structure early in the year, but after May this area of the pond gets very weedy, and it is impossible to find an open area to fish.

FISHERY

This spring pond originally had just a native brook trout population. However, brown trout migrated to the pond from plantings that were made at one time in Elvoy Creek. At the present time it appears that the native brook trout still have a firm hold in this pond, although there are some large browns present. This pond also contains a number of suckers, minnows, and an occasional perch or sunfish. These fish species have migrated from small lakes connected to Elvoy Creek through feeder creeks.

Elvoy Spring Pond has produced some sizeable trout over the years. I can attest to this after having my leader broken three times in one year by some very large trout. One of these trout was approximately 18-20 inches in length. Personally, I have viewed browns that were caught in the 16-18 inch size class and some of both species in the 12-14 inch class. The small trout in this pond are protected due to a minimum size limit of 8 inches for brook trout and 12 inches for brown trout.

In the early days, of course, this pond was quite remote. After discussing this pond with a few local second and third generation Kentucky descendants, it appears that trout fishers in the early part of this century could only reach the pond by hiking in from the county highway. Brook trout were caught up to 20 inches in length in those days by the father of one these men I talked with. Some of these trout were caught through the ice in the middle of winter!

Many of the fingerlings in the pond can be found around the area where the inlet enters. Often you can see brook trout fingerlings feeding on midges around the inlet. Some of the spawning in this pond may take place in this area where there is a great amount of spring seepage. Spawning probably occurs along the gravelly south shore as well.

Also, there are summer evenings when the pond is alive with surface feeding. At this time of the day the larger trout start feeding. These are the magical moments that are cherished by the dry fly fisher.

TACTICS

Elvoy Spring Pond has several hatches of different aquatic insects throughout the season, but the midge hatches are the most abundant. Therefore, when the midge hatch is on, the fly fisher should try a Griffith's Gnat or Chironimid Pupa in sizes 16-22. One particular midge hatch occurred in the middle of the morning one opening day and produced 12 consecutive trout for me without moving a step.

When no midge hatches are occurring, I search the water with a Gold Ribbed Hares Ear Nymph or a black Woolly Bugger in sizes 8-10. The Woolly Bugger simulates a leech's undulating motion. Both flies have produced sizeable trout. Also, early in the season there are a tremendous number of small tadpoles in the shallow parts of the pond. A small, plump black fly with a little tail that has been dubbed the Tadpole Fly has been effective when imitating tadpoles.

Spin fishers will want to try Mepps spinners in various colors or small Rapalas. These lures should imitate the large number of minnows and small suckers present in the pond. On a warm summer night a few years ago, I can remember a man casting off the north bank of the pond and catching and releasing several brookies with a Mepps 00 spinner.

DIRECTIONS

Drive west out of Nelma on County Hwy. A to Fishel Road, then turn left and cross Elvoy Creek and travel past the rustic road turnoff, which is on your left. Proceed on Fishel Road a little further until you see a sand road on the right. Follow this unmarked road down to the parking area.

QUADRANGLE MAP: SMOKY LAKE

BRULE SPRING POND

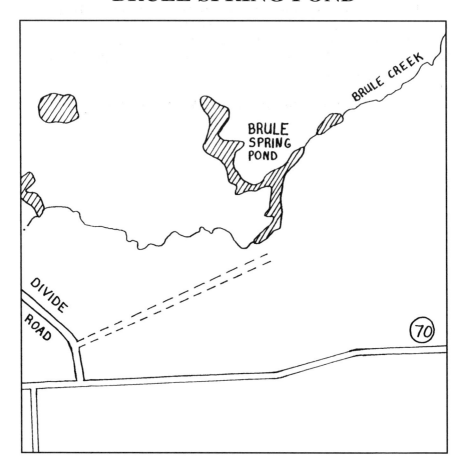

FOREST COUNTY

AREA: 11 ACRES

MAXIMUM DEPTH: 8 FEET

OBSERVATIONS

This large and irregularly shaped spring pond forms the headwaters of Brule Creek and is also part of the Nicolet National Forest. In 1994, Brule Spring Pond was dredged. Therefore, this pond will be in transition for a few more years and may not be very productive for a while.

Brule Spring Pond is surrounded by tamaracks, alders, and marsh grass. At the southern tip of the pond there is a small, flowing inlet with plenty of gravel. This inlet provides extra spawning area for the brook trout residing in the pond. A medium-sized outlet is present on the northeast end of the pond but has experienced some beaver damming. The outlet marks the beginning of Brule Creek which is a brook trout stream. The bottom substrates have changed appreciably due to the pond being dredged. Less muck is present and more sand, marl, and gravel is now exposed. Also, the weed growth is not as heavy as it once was before dredging occurred.

FISHERY

The native brook trout population had declined over the past several years due in part to the pond filling in. Therefore, the pond was hydraulically dredged to increase its carrying capacity and to provide better spawning grounds for the native brook trout present in this system. Generally, this process takes a few years to see results, but in the long run Brule Spring Pond will develop a greater population of brook trout.

The minimum size limit for brook trout in this pond is 7 inches. Possibly raising the limit to 8 inches would protect more spawning age trout and allow the population to expand at a faster rate.

Brule Spring Pond has always had an enormous population of minnows which have provided forage for the larger brookies. It appears that dredging did not reduce the minnow population to any great extent. However, the benthic organisms were most likely reduced in number, and it will probably take some time before recolonization takes place. Most likely this will in turn affect the growth rate of the brook trout population for a period of time.

TACTICS

It is best at the present time to use barbless, artificial lures while the pond is in a transition period. Releasing all brook trout back to the pond should be the angler's number one concern. This will help the brook trout population grow at a quicker pace.

Once again, fly fishers will want to use patterns such as a Griffith's Gnat or a Chironimid Pupa when the brookies are midging. Brookies can be found midging on dropoffs right next to dense weed beds. Also, over deeper parts of the pond, try a Blacknose Dace to imitate the minnow life present in the pond. I would also try a bucktail or streamer anywhere logs jut out into the water from the shoreline or deep undercuts. These are the areas that the brook trout use as shelter.

Spin fishers should try a flashy type of spinner in this dark stained water. Possibly use a silver or fluorescent colored spinner to catch the attention of a brookie.

DIRECTIONS

Drive east of Eagle River on Hwy. 70 until you reach Divide Road, then turn left and take the first unmarked road to the right. This will take you directly to the pond.

QUADRANGLE MAP: ALVIN NW

HOGELEE SPRING POND NO. 1

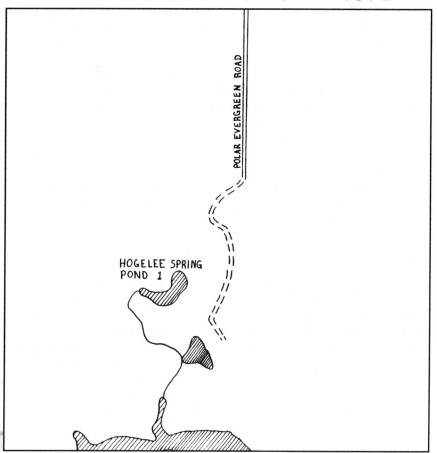

LANGLADE COUNTY

AREA: 2 1/2 ACRES

MAXIMUM DEPTH: 8 FEET

OBSERVATIONS

    Hogelee Spring Pond No. 1 is nestled in a cedar swamp and is located on state owned land. In fact, many of the best ponds in Langlade County are state owned. This spring pond is part of a large complex of spring ponds often referred to as Woods Flowage. Hogelee Spring Pond No. 1 is situated at the top of this complex. The outlet of this pond is located on the west end and connects with the outlet of its twin pond, Hogelee Spring Pond No. 2, which will be discussed later. Then the outlet flows into the west end of Woods Flowage. There appears to be no visible inlet. However, there is a tremendous amount of spring seepage.

There are bountiful supplies of gravel for spawning purposes on the south and west shores. The upper end of the pond will become choked with weeds during the summer. The deeper water in this pond is found over the middle and lower sections. Also, the lower north shore has steep undercuts.

Hogelee Spring Pond No. 1, like many state owned spring ponds in Langlade County, has been hydraulically dredged to improve the carrying capacity of the pond. This particular spring pond was dredged in the late 1960s and is still very productive.

FISHERY

There is a sizeable population of native brook trout in Hogelee Spring Pond No. 1, although there are not that many large trout. This may be due to the 8-inch minimum size limit and bag limit of three trout. Those that fish this pond often use worms and keep most brookies they catch over 8 inches, thus leaving many small trout in the pond. The size range for the brook trout caught in this pond is 4-12 inches in length. However, the majority of the brookies are 5-7 inches in length. Occasionally, you will catch one over 12 inches. Generally, these are very colorful and come from the deep undercuts.

The brook trout in this spring pond have very little competition from other fish species due to the water being so extremely cold. Generally, those spring ponds with the coldest of water will have the least variety of fish species.

TACTICS

Hogelee Spring Pond No. 1 and other spring ponds surrounding this area have for a long time been popular among those interested in spring pond fishing. Although there are not that many people that fly fish on these spring ponds at the present time, I have met a few fly fishers on these spring ponds over the years. Due to the limited amount of time that fly fishers spend on spring ponds, there is a lot of interesting experimentation a fly fisher can do on these ponds. There are large numbers of scuds, chironimids, and caddis in these ponds. I prefer to cast a size 12 weighted nymph to the edges of the pond from a small canoe. Many small brookies will pop out from beneath submerged logs to intercept the nymph offering. Also, you can sink a nymph into the deepest parts of the pond and use a slow hand-twist retrieve. During the day, look for sporadic midge hatches. These midday hatches at times can be quite productive.

As mentioned in Chapter 5, spring ponds in Langlade County and Mepps spinners go hand in hand. The Mepps company is located about 15 miles from the Woods Flowage area in the city of Antigo. Due to the company's close proximity to so many fine spring ponds, there became a loyal following of dedicated spin fishers using Mepps spinners on the spring ponds of this area. Many of these anglers have been quite successful fishing these spring ponds for native brookies.

DIRECTIONS

Drive east of Antigo on Hwy. 64 to Polar-Evergreen Road, then turn right and drive all the way to the parking area by staying to the right. The two-track road at the end is a little bumpy. At the parking lot, you can hike in on a well-traveled trail.

QUADRANGLE MAP: POLAR

HOGELEE SPRING POND NO. 2

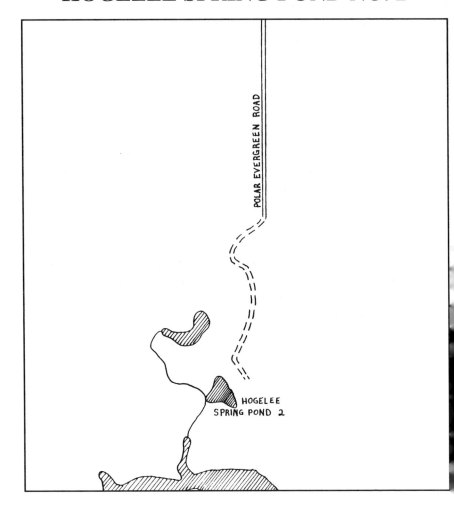

LANGLADE COUNTY

AREA: 2 ACRES

MAXIMUM DEPTH: 8 FEET

OBSERVATIONS

This spring pond is located in the same cedar swamp as its twin, Hogelee Spring Pond No. 1. The outlet, which is fairly large, flows from the west end of the pond. Hogelee Spring Pond No. 2 does not appear to have an inlet, but there is plenty of spring seepage in and around the pond. Of the many spring ponds I have researched and documented from around the state, this spring pond has one of the largest spawning areas for its size. This may account for the large number of small brookies residing in this spring pond. Also, I believe the outlet provides substantial spawning grounds as well.

Hogelee Spring Pond No. 2 was hydraulically dredged along with its twin pond in the late 1960s. It is an extremely productive spring pond from a coldwater fishery standpoint. The productivity of this spring pond is linked to its dense weed beds and numerous logs. Due to these two factors, there is a tremendous number of aquatic food organisms in this pond. These aquatic invertebrates provide a steady supply of food for the brook trout present in the pond.

FISHERY

The brook trout population in this spring pond is considered very healthy, but the average size is quite small. There are several variables which create this large population of small brookies. First, due to a bag limit of three trout and a minimum size limit of 8 inches, the smaller trout in the pond are protected. However, due to these state regulations and the allowance of bait use, there may be some mortality from anglers deep hooking small trout. This in itself, however, will not appreciably reduce the population of brook trout in the pond. Secondly, as mentioned above, there are generous supplies of spawning gravel in the pond and outlet. These facts coupled with ample living space in the pond provide the necessary ingredients for a large population of small trout.

There are some brookies in the 9-12 inch size range in this spring pond, but they are not very common. Most of the trout caught will be in the 4-8 inch size range. So if you like to catch a lot of small brookies, then this pond will be right up your alley.

TACTICS

I like to be fly fishing on this spring pond early in the morning when the mist is rising and the brookies start feeding. Once again, I like to cast toward the shore from a small canoe. My preference is to cast a size 12 Gold Ribbed Hares Ear Nymph between the submerged logs on the east shore. There will be times that it appears the brookies are everywhere. Also, I occasionally probe the deeper water with a nymph and a hand-twist retrieve for the larger brookies in this pond. I have caught several brook trout greater than 10 inches in length using this method over the years.

In many of the spring ponds of this area, the midge hatches are quite common. I have enjoyed some interesting fly fishing with a Griffith's Gnat over the middle of the pond during various times of the day. However, this type of fishing does not always last for a long period of time.

Spin fishers will enjoy success with a Mepps 00 in various colors. Experiment with colors until you find the right one. Color will often matter when it comes to the time of day, the clarity of the water, or the weather that is occurring.

DIRECTIONS

Follow the same directions as those given for Hogelee Spring Pond No. 1.

QUADRANGLE MAP: POLAR

HOGLOT SPRING POND

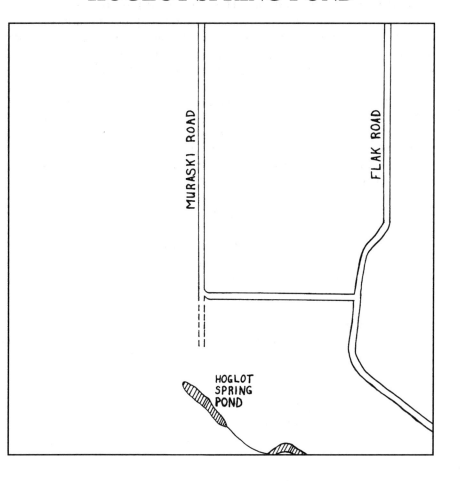

LANGLADE COUNTY

AREA: 1 ACRE

MAXIMUM DEPTH: 5 FEET

OBSERVATIONS

Hoglot Spring Pond feeds into the east end of Woods Flowage. This spring pond has also been dredged and is located in the Woods Flowage State Fishery Area. The pond stretches from northwest to southeast and is small and narrow.

The outlet, which flows out the south end, has had problems in the past with beaver damming. The pond itself has an average amount of spawning gravel, but the outlet has spawning areas as well. However, the problem that arises is that the latter are not available to brook trout residing in the pond, because they are blocked from migrating to the spawning grounds in the outlet.

This narrow spring pond has many of the same landscape features as the last two ponds that were discussed. Also, there is no inlet present. The five spring ponds which feed into the northern side of Woods Flowage all have this characteristic in common. However, all of these spring ponds are generously surrounded by tremendous inflows of spring seepage.

FISHERY

Hoglot Spring Pond does not appear to have as much angling pressure as the Hogelee Spring Ponds do. This in part may be due to its small size. Anglers may be drawn to other ponds in the area which are larger in the hope of catching larger trout. Larger ponds, however, do not always produce larger trout. As mentioned several times in this book, there are many variables which determine the productivity of a spring pond.

Like most spring ponds in this area of the state, it is strictly a native brook trout fishery. There are a 7-inch minimum size limit and a five trout daily bag limit for this spring pond. For this particular spring pond, I would agree with these regulations. One reason these regulations are not harmful to this pond is that the pond is narrow and difficult to fish. Another reason, as mentioned above, is that it does not receive a great amount of pressure from the trout fishing community. Most people who fish this spring pond are local folks.

TACTICS

Most anglers will use bait on Hoglot Spring Pond. Thus, as far as the fly fisher should be concerned, the brookies in this pond are somewhat uneducated. However, this does not mean that catching these native brookies will be easy. One who wants to fly fish on this spring pond will have to deal with being hemmed in by brush. Short direct casts and rollcasting is a must for the fly fisher. I would doubt that the pattern the fly fisher tries will make much difference, except when the brookies may be honed in on midges. Also, try the pond early or late in the day, but don't forget that the best time will probably be when it is raining.

Spin fishers should keep their line as light as possible. The smallest of spinners when cast very softly will produce the best results. Whether spin fishing or fly fishing, keep a low profile and proceed cautiously.

DIRECTIONS

Drive east of Antigo on Hwy. 64 past Polar-Evergreen Road and then turn right on the next road. This is Muraski Road. Follow this road until it bends to the left, then immediately after the bend turn onto the dirt road to the right and follow this into the state fishery area. At the first bend in the dirt road the angler should locate a path that will lead to the spring pond.

QUADRANGLE MAP: POLAR

NIXON SPRING POND

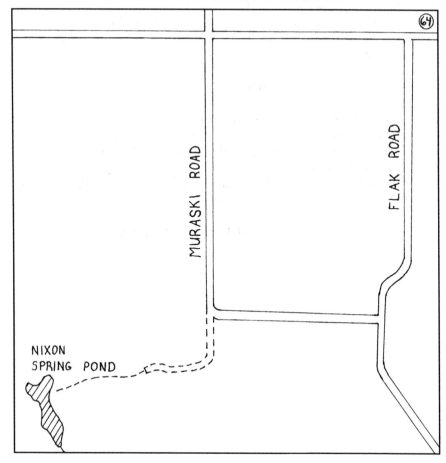

LANGLADE COUNTY

AREA: 2 ACRES

MAXIMUM DEPTH: 8 FEET

OBSERVATIONS

Nixon Spring Pond is also part of the Woods Flowage Complex. It is one of five major spring ponds which feeds into the north side of the flowage. The outlet of Nixon Spring Pond flows out the southern tip of the pond and is congested with debris from old tamaracks that have fallen into the water over time. Like the other spring ponds which feed the flowage from the north, it has no inlet.

Nixon Spring Pond has very dark water over the deeper areas, and the water is extremely cold. The overall depth of this spring pond is excellent, and there are very few shallow areas in this spring pond.

FISHERY

Due to the extremely cold water temperatures in the spring ponds found in the Woods Flowage Complex, native brook trout thrive quite well in these ponds. One factor which may limit the number of brook trout in Nixon Spring Pond is the availability of spawning grounds. However, this could be offset by an influx of brook trout entering through the outlet from Woods Flowage.

Schools of chubs and shiners are quite thick in Nixon Spring Pond. Being that this spring pond has such extremely cold water, it is odd that there are such large numbers of these minnows present. Generally, I have found very few chubs and shiners in those spring ponds with the coldest water temperatures. Usually, the brook stickleback is found in these icy, cold ponds along with the native brook trout. Possibly, the number of adult brook trout present in this pond is not large enough to control the minnow population.

Being that Nixon Spring Pond is somewhat accessible, anglers probably take their toll on the adult brook trout population. This spring pond like the Hogelee Spring Ponds has an 8-inch size limit and three trout daily bag limit. Most anglers use live bait when fishing this spring pond and keep all the brookies they catch over the size limit.

TACTICS

If the angler chooses to fly fish, it is best to do so from a canoe. A canoe can be put in at the northern access point where you will enter from. The fly fisher will find that a size 10 Gold Ribbed Hares Ear Nymph works quite well when the angler casts the fly into deep water and retrieves it back to the shallows. With the number of minnows present in this pond, the fly fisher may wish to try this same technique with a Blacknose Dace Bucktail. If the fly angler chooses to cast to the shallowest parts of the pond, chubs and shiners will pester your fly endlessly.

Fishing a size 18 Griffith's Gnat early and late in the day can also be effective. However, minnows feed quite heavily in this spring pond on midges too. Therefore, the angler should cast with a midge pattern when the brookies are most apt to be midging. This will generally be during low light conditions such as the early morning and evening hours. Keep in mind that minnows seem to feed at any time of the day near the surface.

Spin fishers should try small spinners which are flashy and grab the attention of the trout in the deeper parts of the pond. A small sinking Rapala can also be effective when worked along the undercuts or deeper parts of the pond.

DIRECTIONS

Drive east of Antigo to Muraski Road which is approximately four miles from the town of Polar. Turn right on Muraski Road and follow this road until you come to the first bend. Immediately after the bend in the road turn right and follow this dirt road to the parking area. From here you must carry your canoe or boat down to the pond.

QUADRANGLE MAP: POLAR

RABE SPRING POND

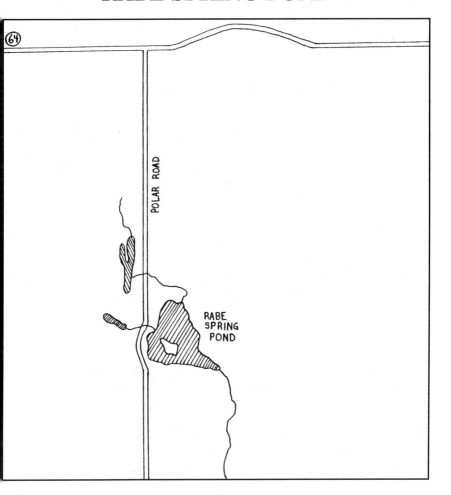

LANGLADE COUNTY

AREA: 6 1/2 ACRES

MAXIMUM DEPTH: 11 FEET

OBSERVATIONS

Rabe Spring Pond has better than average size and depth. However, this state owned pond is missing one important ingredient, spawning areas, that would definitely increase its productivity as a trout fishery. This spring pond was dredged many years ago, but there was no improvement in the pond as far as spawning areas are concerned. The natural makeup of the pond is such that there appears to have been little, if any, spawning grounds ever present within the pond.

Although the pond is pretty much devoid of spawning grounds, it does have two inlets which must provide spawning grounds and recruitment of native brook trout. The inlet flowing in on the west side is the outlet of Krause Spring Pond. This inlet just might be the most important link to sustaining a small native trout population in this spring pond due to the spawning gravel that is present. There is, also, an inlet that enters from the north end. This inlet begins at a spring fed hatchery. An outlet, Rabe Creek, is present at the southeast corner of the pond.

Rabe Spring Pond has a mucky bottom which provides a fertile home for dense beds of weeds. Due to these dense weed beds, there is a rich supply of aquatic invertebrates living in this spring pond. I would assume, however, that the supply of aquatic invertebrates far outweighs the food demands needed for this small population of trout.

FISHERY

As mentioned above, Rabe Spring Pond does harbor a small but sustainable native brook trout population due to the spawning grounds present in its inlets. This pond is also supplemented with hatchery rainbows. This is a questionable practice and one I am sure that came about due to pressure put on the state by trout anglers not happy with the amount of trout that were present in this pond. However, it is not a good practice to plant nonnative species in a spring pond where native species are already present, even though the trout population may be small to start with.

With the state changing its practice of stocking hatchery trout to that of stocking wild trout, I would like to see brook trout transferred from nearby ponds with dense numbers of small brookies to ponds such as Rabe Spring Pond which lack sufficient numbers of trout. Transferring native brook trout from a spring pond with a healthy number of trout to a pond with very few native brook trout makes more sense than planting deformed hatchery rainbows which are out of their element.

TACTICS

Rabe Spring Pond is very easy to gain access to. There is a parking place and boat ramp right off Polar Road. Most people put a small boat or canoe in at this ramp and row or paddle around the pond. Due to the easy access, it may be wise to reduce the bag limit and increase the size limit like some of the other state ponds in the area.

Once again, midge hatches will be important to the fly fisher. Look for trout working the edges of deep weed beds. A Griffith's Gnat in sizes 16-20 will do the job during a midge hatch. This pond has dark water, and an attractor fly at times may be the ticket to locating trout. You may want to go deep in the summer with a size 10 Woolly Bugger, but be prepared to remove weeds occasionally from your fly.

Those who choose to use spinning gear may want to try a flashy color to attract trout in this dark water. There are a number of minnows present in the pond and some bait fishers use minnows.

DIRECTIONS

Drive east of Antigo on Hwy. 64 to Polar, then turn right and travel about two miles. Rabe Spring Pond will be on the left side of the road.

QUADRANGLE MAP: POLAR

KRAUSE SPRING POND

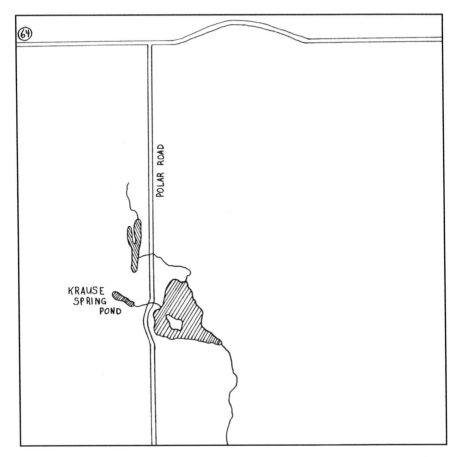

LANGLADE COUNTY

AREA: 1 ACRE

MAXIMUM DEPTH: 11 FEET

OBSERVATIONS

This spring pond, as mentioned earlier, connects to Rabe Spring Pond via an outlet on the east side. Krause Spring Pond is another state owned pond in Langlade County that has been hydraulically dredged.

Krause Spring Pond is surrounded by alders and evergreens. During the summer, it appears that the water gets somewhat murky.

The weed growth in Krause Spring Pond, however, is not as prolific as that of some of the other spring ponds in the area.

Due to the pond being dredged, it does have good depth. There is some spawning gravel present in the pond, but not like the quantity found in most of the spring ponds in the Woods Flowage area.

FISHERY

On one of my last visits to this pond, it appeared that the outlet had been blocked with rocks and wood by someone trying to increase the depth of the pond. Blocking the outlet is plainly detrimental to the fishery, because the gravel in the outlet will be off limits during the spawning season for the brook trout residing in Krause Spring Pond. Also, the temperature near the surface will increase and the ground water inflow will decrease. Most likely the overall population may decrease in the long run if this damming continues.

The population of brook trout in this spring pond is not very large, and the damming discussed above does not help the situation. Also, the few brookies that are caught will, generally, be on the small side. Even though the brookies are few and somewhat small, the aesthetic value is very high due to the quiet, wooded setting surrounding this little pond.

TACTICS

It is very difficult to fly cast on this small pond. A fly fisher will need to be proficient at rollcasting due to being walled in with trees and brush. These uneducated but spooky trout require a quiet approach. Any nymph pattern in sizes 12-16 will fill the ticket if you can make the proper cast. Try this pond on a drizzly, overcast day when you can get closer to the trout.

Spin fishers will have a much better chance on this pond. This is because spin fishers will be able to cast long distances without the fear of brush catching their backcast. Casting small Mepps spinners tied onto 2-pound test line will produce several brookies on a good day.

DIRECTIONS

Look for a trail to Krause Spring Pond right across the road from Rabe Spring Pond.

QUADRANGLE MAP: POLAR

TOWN LINE SPRING POND

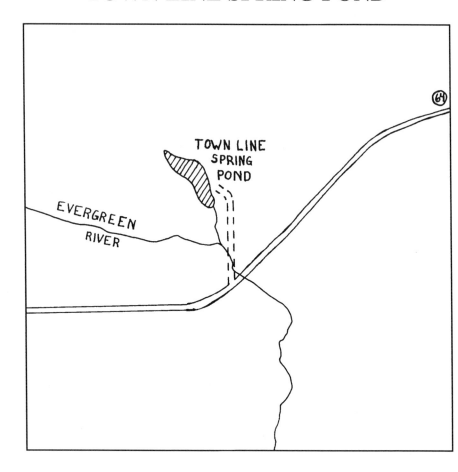

LANGLADE COUNTY

AREA: 3 ACRES

MAXIMUM DEPTH: 7 FEET

OBSERVATIONS

Town Line Spring Pond is owned by the state and is very accessible. The upper end of the pond lies in a cedar and tamarack studded swamp. There is an open area on the northeast shore, but the majority of the lower part has alders as a border. This spring pond is connected to the Evergreen River through a short outlet. The outlet, which flows out of the southeast corner of the pond, has had a history of being dammed by beavers. Presently, the outlet is being kept open. This is highly beneficial, because I would suspect that the outlet plays a vital role in the number of trout that are present in this pond.

Like many of the spring ponds in this area, it does not have an inlet. However, as mentioned above, the outlet of this pond probably holds the key to the number of trout present in this pond. In certain parts of this spring pond, the bottom does have gravel and coarse sand in which the trout may spawn. This also may be a major contributor to the trout productivity in this spring pond. The rest of the pond has a bottom composed of muck, rocks, and marl. It appears that the upper and middle sections hold the greatest depths in this spring pond. Town Line Spring Pond has a decent average depth for maintaining a good number of trout.

FISHERY

The Evergreen area has had an interesting past. My grandfather fished for brook trout, camped, and stayed with local friends of Kentucky descent back in the 1920s and 1930s in the Evergreen area. During this time period, interesting stories involving the locals and game wardens have come out of this area. In the early part of this century, locals were often scrutinized by game wardens. This is because locals would often seek brook trout and other wild game during the closed season. In the winter, this often meant icefishing on the area ponds for native brookies.

During this era, food and money were hard to come by. Locals would obtain food for their families by any means possible, even if it meant breaking the law. However, the game wardens had a job to do, and this meant controlling poaching wherever they could. It would have been very difficult during that time period to take a position in this conflict of interests, when one side was fighting for survival while the other side was trying to protect the natural resources of the Evergreen area.

The section of the Evergreen River adjacent to Town Line Spring Pond is class 1 trout water with an incredible supply of spawning gravel. Due to the large number of trout reproduced in this section of the Evergreen River, there is a good possibility that a number of these trout make there way into the pond through the outlet.

As mentioned above, I believe that the outlet plays a major role in the trout fishery present in this pond. Therefore, the number one concern is to maintain an open channel from the pond to the river. Also, being that this pond is one of the most accessible of the state owned ponds in Langlade County, it might be wise to change the three trout bag limit and 8-inch minimum size limit for brook trout and 12-inch minimum size limit for brown trout to artificial lures only with a larger size limit and reduced bag limit like that found on Blue Spring Pond which connects to the Hunting River in northern Langlade County.

Although native brook trout are the main emphasis of this book, this spring pond has a mix of brook trout and brown trout. Of course, the methods and techniques used may dictate which type of trout is caught the most often.

As mentioned, browns are present in this spring pond. I assume that the browns first entered Town Line Spring Pond through the outlet after populations became established earlier in this century in the Evergreen River and the Wolf River systems.

TACTICS

It is best to launch a canoe, boat, or float tube at the opening on the northeast shore. The carry down to the pond is not very far. Also, it is possible to walk around the shoreline and fish with spinning equipment.

My fly fishing experiences on this spring pond have not always been positive. This may be due to the rather heavy angling pressure put on this pond. However, during midge hatches, there appears to be a healthy population of trout present in Town Line Spring Pond.

Some very colorful trout have come from the deep undercuts along the north shore. These trout have generally fallen for a weighted Gold Ribbed Hares Ear Nymph in sizes 8-12. For best results, the nymph should land right next to the edge of the under-cut. Midge hatches can produce some interesting fishing over the middle and lower sections of the pond. Chironimid Pupa patterns are effective during midge hatches when placed over feeding trout.

Spin fishers may enjoy success casting to these deep undercuts too. A brass or copper colored spinner may work well to simulate small chubs and shiners present in this pond. Also, try to cast among any submerged logs along the shoreline.

DIRECTIONS

Drive west of Langlade on Hwy. 64 until you cross the Evergreen River, then turn right on Town Line Road. You will cross the Evergreen River again, then proceed until you come to an opening. At this point turn left, and the pond will be on your left side.

QUADRANGLE MAP: WHITE LAKE

EVERGREEN SPRING POND

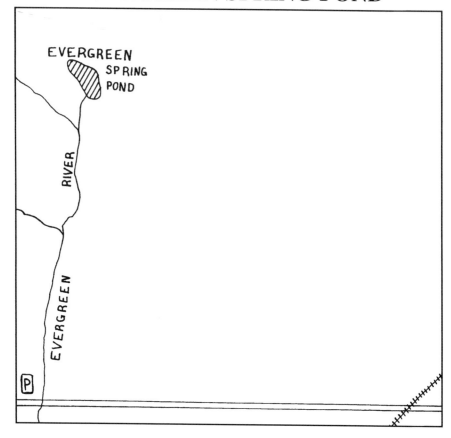

LANGLADE COUNTY

AREA: 1 ACRE

MAXIMUM DEPTH: 5 FEET

OBSERVATIONS

Evergreen Spring Pond is part of the Evergreen River system and is located on state owned land. This spring pond is somewhat remote. To reach Evergreen Spring Pond, you must hike through some brushy country. Also, the land surrounding this area of the Evergreen River is somewhat swampy.

There is a short outlet flowing from the southwest corner of the pond to the Evergreen River. No doubt this small outlet allows trout to enter and exit the pond during certain times of the year.

FISHERY

It is well known that the Evergreen River has produced some nice trout in the past. In the early part of this century, my grandfather would regularly catch 13-14 inch brook trout from this area of the river on down to the reservation. Of course, this was before brown trout were present in the system. Although there are still plenty of brook trout in the Evergreen River and its adjoining spring ponds, the brook trout present in this system will never quite reach the size that they once did due to the presence of brown trout and greater fishing pressure.

Evergreen Spring Pond is remote enough that it offers a quality but difficult trout fishing experience. If you are adventurous and in good enough shape, then give the native brook trout of this spring pond a try.

TACTICS

As mentioned above, be sure you are in good physical condition before making the journey to this pond. There will be some slow going due to the brush and swampland you will traverse.

The fly fisher should be aware that this is not a fly fishing paradise. Be prepared to make short casts. Also, you should be proficient at rollcasting. Keep your leaders light, preferably a 7X leader, and keep a low profile. If you are adept at casting in tight quarters, then your chances are good that you will catch some of the native brook trout residing in this pond. I would suggest fishing this small pond on a dreary, overcast day. These uneducated brookies will hit any nymph in sizes 10-16 if you can present your offering without making too much commotion.

If you are using spinning gear, then you will want to stay with a small spinner like a Mepps 00. Try different colors until you find the one that is the most effective. Keep a low profile, and make soft casts with 2-pound test line.

DIRECTIONS

Drive west of Langlade on Hwy. 64 until you reach County

Hwy. P, then turn left and drive to the second bridge that crosses over the Evergreen River on County Hwy. P. Park next to the river, and hike upstream on the right side of the river. On the hike upstream, you will encounter a feeder stream entering on the left. Keep moving upstream until you see a feeder creek on the right side, then follow this short outlet up to the spring pond. A quadrangle map of the area may be helpful.

QUADRANGLE MAP: WHITE LAKE

This spring pond does not show up on the map. However, you can follow the river up from County Hwy. P on the map, and you will notice a swampy area on the right side of the stream above its confluence with Evergreen Creek. This is where the pond is located.

LOWER JONES SPRING POND

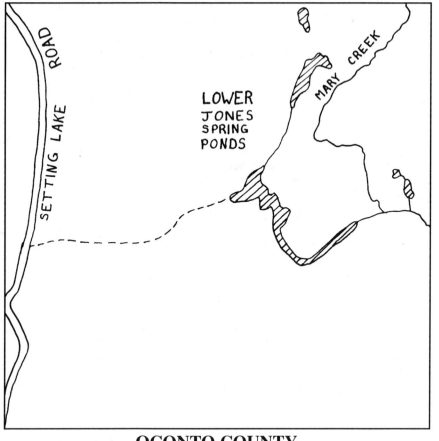

LOWER JONES SPRING PONDS

SETTING LAKE ROAD

MARY CREEK

OCONTO COUNTY

AREA: 3 ACRES

MAXIMUM DEPTH: 6 FEET

OBSERVATIONS

Lower Jones Spring Pond is located in a nonmotorized recreation area known as the Jones Springs Area. This large wilderness tract is situated in the southern part of the Nicolet National Forest. There are 2,000 acres in which you can roam and enjoy the peace and solitude of a quiet northern forest.

The only way to reach Lower Jones Spring Pond is by parking

along the boundary surrounding this recreation area and then hiking into the interior where this spring pond is located. A trail skirts along the northwest portion of the pond. It is here that you may want to try your luck for native brookies.

Evergreens and alders surround the majority of the shoreline. There is a place along the upper end where some anglers have built a campsite. However, this particular spot is not considered a designated camping area. Pick up a brochure on the Jones Springs Area if you wish to camp in a designated area.

Lower Jones Spring Pond has a clear inlet entering from the north. This is the outlet of Upper Jones Spring Pond. The inlet is jammed with many old timbers. Also, this spring pond has a lot of submerged timber along its upper edges. There is not a wealth of spawning gravel in this pond. However, there is a short outlet which feeds Mary Creek. Mary Creek then flows into the South Branch of the Oconto River. Both of these streams have native brook trout and supplies of spawning gravel.

FISHERY

Lower Jones Spring Pond has a lower than average population of native brook trout. However, there is a good possibility that a number of brook trout enter the pond through the outlet. These brook trout may be hatched in Mary Creek. Also, brook trout may transfer back and forth between the two ponds at certain times of the year.

Residing in this lower pond with the brook trout are bluegills and vast numbers of minnows. These species have most likely entered this pond from lakes that are connected to the streams lower down in this system. Warmwater species when present in a spring pond often suggests that part of the year the pond may be marginal habitat for native brook trout due to higher temperature levels.

TACTICS

It is possible to spin fish along the edges of this spring pond. However, it is not practical to fly fish along the edges of Lower Jones Spring Pond. Therefore, being that the hike in is about one-half mile, it is best to carry in a float tube or a very small canoe. Watch for mucky areas if you intend to fish from a float tube. Also, for safety purposes, I would suggest bringing along a fishing partner if you intend to fish from a float tube.

Fly patterns that are highly visible such as a Royal Coachman Wet Fly, a Woolly Bugger, or a Mickey Finn can be used successfully when searching for brookies. Try this pond early in the season when the water is still quite cold. I believe that the water temperature may be too warm during the middle and latter parts of summer to warrant making a fishing trip to this pond.

If you prefer to spin fish, you can cover most of the pond by walking along the shoreline. I would suggest using a flashy spinner that will attract the attention of a brookie in this dark colored pond. Remember that there are an 8-inch minimum size limit and three trout bag limit, although I would hope most people fishing a wild spring pond like this would release most of the trout caught over 8 inches in length.

DIRECTIONS

Drive north and west of Mountain on Hwy. 64 until you reach County Hwy. T, then turn right and drive to Saul Springs Road. Turn left on this road until you reach a "T" intersection, then turn right and stay on Setting Lake Road. You will cross the headwaters of the South Branch of the Oconto River twice, then continue about a mile until you reach a parking area on the right side of the road. You can park here and hike about one-half mile to the lower pond. It is a good idea to obtain a map of the area from the Lakewood Ranger Station on Hwy. 32.

QUADRANGLE MAP: RESERVOIR POND

My grandfather (left) and great uncle on a spring pond outing in 1928

CHAPTER

Eight

A LISTING OF SPRING PONDS

*T*he purpose of this chapter is to provide the trout angler with an extensive list of spring ponds to choose from. I have examined an endless number of maps so that I could compile a large list of spring ponds with names. Although this list of spring ponds is extensive, it is far from complete. There may be some named spring ponds that have been missed. Also, as mentioned earlier in this book, there are hundreds of spring ponds in Wisconsin that have been left unnamed due to being small and remote. For the most part, these spring ponds will not be included in this book. I have, however, uncovered a few spring ponds which have local names but remain unnamed on county and quadrangle maps. These spring ponds will be included in this chapter, although they will be difficult for the trout angler to find.

All of the spring ponds in this listing are alphabetized by name within each county. The counties in the state of Wisconsin where spring ponds can be found have also been arranged alphabetically. When searching for spring ponds listed in this chapter, the angler will find some of the larger and more popular ponds on county maps. However, quadrangle maps will be much more helpful in locating the majority of the spring ponds. The angler wishing to use quadrangle maps to locate spring ponds listed in this chapter will have to do so by finding the appropriate quadrangle maps within each county. As mentioned in Chapter 2, the angler can purchase quadrangle maps from the USGS, map companies, and outdoor specialty stores. Appendix II in the back of this book is a listing of map companies which sell quadrangle maps. Quadrangle maps can help the angler locate some of the smaller spring ponds which do not show up on any other type of map. Many of these ponds lie in remote swamps and may not see a trout angler all season long. Those anglers with an adventurous spirit may wish to locate one or more of these remote ponds.

Each spring pond has also been categorized as private or public. However, it should be acknowledged that ownership of a spring pond can change hands. In fact, the DNR has acquired many spring ponds from private holdings over the last several years. Therefore, if the angler is in doubt whether a pond is private or public, an up to date county plat book will be a valuable resource for determining the present status of a given pond.

Spring ponds designated as public are those ponds which are situated on federal, state, or county land. Because public spring ponds are open for fishing to all trout anglers, these are the ponds an angler should try to locate first. There are many walk-in trails on federal and state lands which lead directly to spring ponds. Those trails leading over public land make locating spring ponds a much easier task. On the other hand, some anglers prefer getting off the beaten path. For the angler that prefers a challenge, there are a number of public spring ponds which require a longer hike over unmarked trails and the use of a compass.

A private spring pond is generally one in which the landowner has full control over the land surrounding the pond. The only legal ways for the angler to cross over private land to a spring pond is when the land is under the FCL program or when the landowner has granted permission. There is also one other way of reaching a spring pond on private land. This method involves a spring pond being connected to navigable water. If an angler can navigate a watercraft on a stream from public land through private land to a spring pond without setting foot on the land surrounding the pond, then the angler is within the law granted by Wisconsin's navigable water rights.

However, even if crossing over or through private land can be done legally, it is still a good idea to ask permission of the landowner whenever possible. Building friendly relations with the owner of the land is always advisable.

In this listing, the angler will also find the trout species present within each spring pond. Although the emphasis of this book has been on spring ponds with native or wild brook trout populations, there are a few spring ponds with stocked trout. Also, browns and rainbows will occasionally be found in some spring ponds due to indiscriminate plantings or migrations to a pond from a connecting stream.

There are also a few spring ponds which have marginal water temperatures for trout during the hot days of summer. In spring ponds with marginal water temperatures, warmwater species may mix with the trout population. Generally, these spring ponds will not have dense populations of native trout.

In closing, those anglers that are adventurous will enjoy the quest of finding different spring ponds from year to year. It is hoped that the angler will come to realize that these sparkling gems are a precious resource. In fact, a resource so special that the trout angler will choose to release most or all of the native brook trout caught in these tiny waters. Also, it is hoped that the angler will treat the land surrounding each spring pond with respect, whether it be private or public, and keep the land free of litter. Remember that the future of these magical little trout ponds rests with each and every one of us that enjoys the wonderful world of the native brook trout.

Spring pond reflections

ASHLAND COUNTY

NAME	OWNERSHIP	TROUT SPECIES
Bay	Private	Brook
Kempf	Private	Brook
Kenyon	Private	Brook

BARRON COUNTY

NAME	OWNERSHIP	TROUT SPECIES
Engle Creek	Public	Brook
Vermillion	Private	Brook

BAYFIELD COUNTY

NAME	OWNERSHIP	TROUT SPECIES
Bearsdale	Public	Brook
Bearsdale, Lower	Public	Brook
Blazer Creek	Public	Brook
DeChamps Creek	Public	Brook, Brown
Eighteenmile Creek	Public	Brook, Brown
Fish Creek	Private	Brook
Hyatt	Public	Brook
Johnson	Public	Brook
Shunenberg	Public	Brook
Siskiwit	Public	Brook
White River	Public	Brook, Brown

BURNETT COUNTY

NAME	OWNERSHIP	TROUT SPECIES
Barrens	Private	Brook
Bass Lake	Private	Brook
Clam River	Public	Brook, Brown
Culbertson	Public	Brown
Dogtown	Public	Brook
Nelson	Private	Brook
Spring Creek	Public	Brook, Brown
Twenty-Six Lake	Public	Brook

DOUGLAS COUNTY

NAME	OWNERSHIP	TROUT SPECIES
Beaupre	Public	Brook
Bergen Creek	Public	Brook
Big	Public	Brook
Blue	Public	Brook
Buckley	Public	Brook
Cranberry	Public	Brook
Horseshoe	Private	Brook
McDougal	Public	Brook
Poplar River	Private	Brook, Brown
Spring Creek	Private	Brook

FLORENCE COUNTY

NAME	OWNERSHIP	TROUT SPECIES
Trout	Public	Brook

FOREST COUNTY

NAME	OWNERSHIP	TROUT SPECIES
Brule	Public	Brook
Camp One	Public	Brook
Charlie Otto	Private	Brook
Elvoy	Public	Brook, Brown
Hemlock	Public	Brook
Hoffman	Private	Brook
Huff	Public	Brook
Indian	Public	Brook
Johnson	Public	Brook
Jones	Public	Brook
Marsh No. 10 Creek	Public	Brook
Ninemile	Public	Brook
Otter	Public	Brook
Shawano Creek	Public	Brook
Torpee No. 1	Public	Brook
Torpee No. 2	Public	Brook
Perry	Public	Brook
Zieler	Public	Brook

LANGLADE COUNTY

NAME	OWNERSHIP	TROUT SPECIES
Anderson	Private	Brook
Augustyn	Private	Brook
Bellis	Private	Brook
Blue	Public	Brook, Brown
Campbell	Private	Brook
Chisel	Private	Brook
Clubhouse	Public	Brook, Brown
Deer Creek	Public	Brook
Demlow, Lower	Public	Brook
Demlow, Upper	Public	Brook
Denault	Public	Brook
Drab	Public	Brook
Duck	Public	Brook
Elcho	Private	Brook
Elton	Public	Brook
Elmhurst	Private	Brook
Emil	Public	Brook
Emil, Little	Public	Brook
Evergreen	Public	Brook, Brown
Flood	Private	Brook
Flora	Public	Brook, Brown
Galyan	Private	Brook
Garski	Public	Brook
Hanson	Public	Brook, Brown
Harper	Private	Brook
Hatton	Private	Brook
Heinz	Public	Brook
Heinzen	Private	Brook
Hidden	Private	Brook
Hogelee No. 1	Public	Brook
Hogelee No. 2	Public	Brook
Hoglot	Public	Brook
Homestead	Public	Brook
Karberger	Public	Brook
Kielcheski	Public	Brook
Knoke	Public	Brook
Krause	Public	Brook
Leonard Nixon	Private	Brook
Lily	Public	Brook
Long Lake	Private	Brook
Lost	Private	Brook
Markgraff	Private	Brook

LANGLADE COUNTY(CONTINUED)

NAME	OWNERSHIP	TROUT SPECIES
Martin	Private	Brook
Maxwell	Private	Brook
Mayking	Private	Brook
McCaslin	Public	Brook
Moonshine	Private	Brook
Moose Lake	Public	Brook, Brown
Nixon	Public	Brook
O'Brien, Lower	Private	Brook
O'Brien, Upper	Private	Brook
Ort	Private	Brook
Otter	Private	Brook
Parsons	Private	Brook
Payne	Private	Brook
Pines	Private	Brook
Polar	Public	Brook
Poor Farm	Private	Brook
Punch Out	Private	Brook
Purple	Public	Brook
Rabe	Public	Brook, Rainbow
Rasmussen	Private	Brook
Roix	Private	Brook
Saul	Public	Brook, Brown
Shadick	Public	Brook
Sipes	Public	Brook
Spring Lake	Public	Brook
Starks	Public	Brook
Stevens	Private	Brook
Stillhouse	Private	Brook
Strassberg	Private	Brook
Sunshine	Public	Brook, Brown
Thompson	Private	Brook
Tobacco	Public	Brook
Town Line	Public	Brook, Brown
Trout	Public	Brook
Wildcat	Public	Brook
Willow	Public	Brook
Wood Duck	Public	Brook, Brown
Woods	Public	Brook

LINCOLN COUNTY

NAME	OWNERSHIP	TROUT SPECIES
Alta	Public	Brook
King	Public	Brook
Kippenburg	Public	Brook
Kolko	Public	Brook
Spring Lake	Public	Brook
Staub	Public	Brook
Staub, Lower	Private	Brook

MANITOWOC COUNTY

NAME	OWNERSHIP	TROUT SPECIES
Millhome	Public	Brook

MARATHON COUNTY

NAME	OWNERSHIP	TROUT SPECIES
Bear	Public	Brook
Boathouse	Private	Brook
Clark	Public	Brook
Falstad	Private	Brook
Jacobson	Public	Brook
Koepsel	Public	Brook
Raiders	Private	Brook
Silent	Public	Brook
Spiegel	Public	Brook, Brown
Spring Lake	Private	Brook
Totten	Public	Brook, Brown

MARINETTE COUNTY

NAME	OWNERSHIP	TROUT SPECIES
Babson	Private	Brook
Homestead	Private	Brook
Medbrook	Private	Brook

MONROE COUNTY

NAME	OWNERSHIP	TROUT SPECIES
Cataract	Public	Brown
Evans	Public	Brook
Hans Biegel	Public	Brook
Iron	Private	Brook
Swamp	Public(Military)	Brook

OCONTO COUNTY

NAME	OWNERSHIP	TROUT SPECIES
Barney	Private	Brook
Forbes	Public	Brook
Hells Acre	Private	Brook
Hickey	Public	Brook
Jones, Lower	Public	Brook
Jones, Upper	Public	Brook
Sullivan	Public	Brook
Town	Public	Brook

ONEIDA COUNTY

NAME	OWNERSHIP	TROUT SPECIES
Bearskin	Public	Brook
Camp Fifteen	Public	Brook
Cedar	Private	Brook
Goodnow	Public	Brook
Goodyear	Public	Brook
Harshaw	Public	Brook
Heal	Private	Brook
Kitty	Private	Brook
Lamers	Private	Brook
Mercer	Public	Brook
Newbold	Private	Brook
Palm	Private	Brook
Radtke	Private	Brook
Rocky Run	Private	Brook
Scott	Private	Brook
Smallpox	Public	Brook
Spring Creek	Private	Brook
Starks	Private	Brook
Woodboro	Public	Brook
White	Private	Brook

POLK COUNTY

NAME	OWNERSHIP	TROUT SPECIES
Black Brook	Private	Brook
Marquee	Private	Brook
Silver Branch Creek	Public	Brook
Spencer Creek	Private	Brook, Brown
Toby	Private	Brook
Wagon Landing Creek	Public	Brook

PRICE COUNTY

NAME	OWNERSHIP	TROUT SPECIES
Betsy Creek	Private	Brook
Camp C	Public	Brook
Camp Four	Public	Brook
Camp Nine	Public	Brook
Foulds	Public	Brook
Hogsback	Public	Brook
Jackson	Private	Brook
Janacek	Private	Brook
Newman	Public	Brook .
Niebauer	Public	Brook
Ottertail	Private	Brook
Sieverson	Public	Brook
Willow	Public	Brook

ST. CROIX COUNTY

NAME	OWNERSHIP	TROUT SPECIES
Anderson	Private	Brook
Kelly	Private	Brook
Levesque	Private	Brook

SAWYER COUNTY

NAME	OWNERSHIP	TROUT SPECIES
Bean Brook	Public	Brook
Beaver Creek	Private	Brook
Benson	Public	Brook, Brown
Buckhorn	Public	Brook
Bulldog	Public	Brook
Connor	Public	Brook
Dead Creek	Public	Brook
Dead Creek, Lower	Public	Brook
Eddy Creek	Public	Brook
Forty-One Creek	Public	Brook
Graveyard	Public	Brook
Grindstone	Public	Brook
Grindstone, Lower	Public	Brook
Grindstone, Upper	Private	Brook
Hauer	Public	Brook
Hauer, Lower	Private	Brook
Hay	Private	Brook
Knuteson	Private	Brook
Maple	Public	Brook
Mosquito Brook	Public	Brook, Brown
Moss Creek	Private	Brook
Price Creek	Public	Brook
Venison	Public	Brook
Weirgor	Public	Brook, Brown

SHAWANO COUNTY

NAME	OWNERSHIP	TROUT SPECIES
Embarrass	Public	Brook, Brown

VILAS COUNTY

NAME	OWNERSHIP	TROUT SPECIES
Allequash	Public	Brook
Blackjack	Public	Brook
Elvoy	Public	Brook
Garland	Public	Brook
Goodyear	Public	Brook
Haymeadow	Public	Brook
Little Crooked	Private	Brook
McGinnis	Public	Brook
Ontonagon	Public	Brook
Portage	Public	Brook
Rainbow	Private	Brook
Reservoir	Public	Brook
Salsich	Public	Brook
Siphon	Public	Brook
Spring Creek(North)	Private	Brook
Spring Creek(South)	Public	Brook
Springmeadow	Public	Brook
Stevenson	Public	Brook
Sucker Creek	Private	Brook
Tamarack	Public	Brook
Three	Public	Brook
Trout	Public	Brook

WASHBURN COUNTY

NAME	OWNERSHIP	TROUT SPECIES
Bashaw Trout	Private	Brook
Bean Brook	Public	Brook
Beaver Lodge	Public	Brook
Boyle Brook	Public	Brook
Clam River	Public	Brook
Dago Creek	Private	Brook
Earl	Public	Brook
Gull Creek	Public	Brook
Little Mackay Creek	Public	Brook
Mackay	Public	Brook
McKenzie	Public	Brook, Brown
Sawyer Creek	Public	Brook
Spring Creek	Public	Brook
Veazie	Private	Brook
Westenberg	Private	Brook
Whalen Creek	Public	Brook, Brown

WAUKESHA COUNTY

NAME	**OWNERSHIP**	**TROUT SPECIES**
McClintock	Public	Brook, Brown
Paradise	Public	Brook, Brown

WAUSHARA COUNTY

NAME	**OWNERSHIP**	**TROUT SPECIES**
Cedar	Public	Brook
Fenrich	Private	Brook, Brown
Mecan	Public	Brown

APPENDIX I
FLY AND TACKLE SHOPS

The Fly Fishers
8601 West Greenfield Avenue
West Allis, WI 53214
(414) 259-8100

Eagle Sports
702 Wall Street
Eagle River, WI 54521
(715) 479-8804

The Flyshop at Bob's
1504 Velp Avenue
Green Bay, WI 54303
1-800-447-2312

Bill Sherer's We Tie It
P.O. Box 516
Boulder Junction, WI 54512
(715) 385-0171

Sheldon's, Inc.-Mepps(Guided Tours)
626 Center Street
Antigo, WI 54409

Mike's Mobil Service
Junction Hwys. 55 & 64 in
Langlade
White Lake, WI 54491
(715) 882-8901

Wolf River Fly Shop
N4216 Rocky Rips Road
White Lake, WI 54491
(715) 882-5941

Fishful Thinking Fly Shop
N3494 Hwy. 55
White Lake, WI 54491
(715) 882-3474

Ace Hardware
500 E. Ashland Avenue
Appleton, WI 54911
(414) 731-0500

Fontana Sports Specialties
6670 Odana Road
Madison, WI 53701
(608) 833-0678

Anglers All
2803 Lakeshore Drive
Ashland, WI 54802
(715) 682-5754

Lunde's Fly Fishing Chalet
2491 Highway 92
Mt. Horeb, WI 53572
(608) 437-5465

Laacke and Joys
1433 N. Water Street
Milwaukee, WI 53202
(414) 271-7878

Spring Creek Angler
P.O. Box 283
Coon Valley, WI 54623
(608) 452-3430

Brule River Classics
P.O. Box 306
Brule, WI 54820
(715) 372-8153

Phoenix Company(Poke Boat)
Berea, KY 40403
(606) 986-2336

APPENDIX II
MAP COMPANIES

Clarkson Map Company
1225 Delanglade Street
Kaukauna, WI 54130
(414) 766-3000

Wall Hangers LTD., Inc.
N9274 C.T.H. X
Black Creek, WI 54106

SUGGESTED READINGS

Borger, Gary. 1979. Nymphing. Stackpole Books, Harrisburg.

Brynildson, Oscar and Robert Carline. 1977. Effects of hydraulic dredging on the ecology of native trout populations in Wisconsin spring ponds. Technical Bulletin No. 98, Wisconsin Department of Natural Resources, Madison.

Cordes, Ron and Randall Kaufmann. 1984. Lake Fishing With a Fly. Frank Amato Publications, Portland.

Hughes, Dave. 1991. Strategies for Stillwater. Stackpole Books, Harrisburg.

LaFontaine, Gary. 1981. Caddisflies. Lyons and Burford, New York.

Mueller, Ross. 1995. Upper Midwest Flies That Catch Trout and How to Fish Them. R. Mueller Publications, Appleton.

Schwiebert, Ernest. 1955. Matching the Hatch. MacMillan, New York.